D1560432

BASSETT-LOWKE

WATERLINE SHIP MODELS

DEREK HEAD

Golden Age Editions

⚊ TO ANNE ⚊

First edition published in Great Britain by Golden Age Editions, 1996.
Limited edition of 1000 copies.
Golden Age Editions is an imprint of New Cavendish Books Ltd.

Publisher and Editor – Narisa Chakra
Design and Typesetting – John B Cooper
Art direction – Supadee Ruangsak
Photography – Mark Williams
Project consultant – Allen Levy

Printed and bound in Thailand at Eastern Printing (Public) Company.

Golden Age Editions, 3 Denbigh Road, London W11 2SJ

ISBN: 1 872727 72 7

❧ CONTENTS ❧

FOREWORD

To anyone who was a child or had children of their own between the 1920s and the 1950s, the name Bassett-Lowke meant something very special, a name to be spoken of in almost reverential tones. A whispered "it's a Bassett-Lowke," would somehow signify the ultimate seal of approval for the object under scrutiny, and what objects they were too!

Beautifully and lovingly crafted replicas of railway engines and ships in many different scales, some up to 20 feet long and others a mere inch or two.

What joy and pride they gave to those lucky enough to own one and how many small, and indeed not so small, pairs of eyes of those who were less fortunate, gazed in wonder and longing at the models displayed at exhibitions or in the windows of well-known railway and steamship companies' offices, or indeed in Bassett-Lowke's own retail outlets.

Moreover, it was not just the public who held the name in awe. I well recall the late Percy Claydon, a former joint managing director of the company with responsibility for the ship side of the business, relating a true story concerning a representative from a reasonably well-known company, who had gone to Liverpool to visit the head of public relations of Cunard Line – "the meanest shipping company and very autocratic" – to use his own words! The rep had been kept waiting all day and had been forced to find somewhere to stay overnight. The following day he was again seated in the waiting-room and was somewhat taken aback when two gentlemen arrived and were ushered straight in. On enquiring why he was kept waiting and others were not, he was coolly informed that – "It all depends on the name of the firm, Sir." The two gentlemen, needless to say, were from Bassett-Lowke!

Derek Head has been a collector of Bassett-Lowke waterline ship models for about 60 years. In writing this book, which is devoted solely to the miniature ship models that B-L turned out by the thousand during the first half of this century, he shares with us not only his intimate knowlege of the subject but also his great love of these miniature replicas that so accurately mimicked their full-sized ocean-going counterparts.

I congratulate him on his effort and feel sure that all who read this book and enjoy its pictures will also share some of his enthusiasm for these little treasures of past times.

LORD GREENWAY

3. *The painting by J Seymour Lucas titled 'A New Whip for the Dutch', held by the Victoria & Albert Museum in London, illustrates the use of a model three-dimensionally to demonstrate the characteristics of a ship in the 17th century.*

～ INTRODUCTION ～

The art of model-making can be traced back to pre-historic times, whether it be the making of facsimiles of men and animals or creating effigies of gods and goddesses. Likewise the advent of model ships dates back to the earliest civilisation, since man has always been closely involved with the sea.

Not only does the construction of a model give satisfaction and pleasure to its creator but it also meets man's deepfelt desire to possess, in miniature form, a replica of some object of special significance. A model has the advantage that it is usually manageable and can be easily handled, displayed or stored, which is especially important when considering objects such as ships or other floating craft of one sort or another.

The world of the model ranges from objets d'art created by Fabergé, where the most intricate and delicate of work can be admired and appreciated by all, to the robust but simple rocking-horse, that allows a child's imagination to transport a 'real' pony into the nursery. Technical and professional models enable the designer or planner to make proposals to a prospective client in a three dimensional way, whether the subject be architectural, marine or otherwise.

Throughout this century and even earlier, the toy industry has relied on models in one form or another to satisfy the demands of both adults and children. The concept of war gaming, which relies heavily on the use of miniature replicas and which from time immemorial has been the sole province of the military, has recently become a growing pastime enjoyed by members of the general public.

Mementoes and souvenirs have always been an attractive proposition for model-makers, who have seldom missed opportunities to capitalise on the public –

or official – wish to commemorate events of special significance: for instance models of the coronation coach or a record-breaking boat, car, plane or train.

The British Board of Admiralty has, for many centuries, used models to illustrate new proposals for men-of-war, models which have superseded their original practical role to become works of art in their own right. The accuracy and quality of these old ship models, created by skilled craftsmen over the last two or three hundred years, makes such objects highly desirable today and those which survive fetch very high prices when they appear on the market. Many now grace some of the finest maritime museums around the world.

It is difficult to establish accurately when ship models were first used for practical purposes but there are many records of hull models produced for the Royal Navy for training purposes towards the end of the last century. These were either full or part models and were designed for specific teaching or demonstration purposes, such as the arrangement of sails or rigging, deck layout and boat handling and stowage of anchors and cables. Similar aids were also used in the merchant navy training schools but with the addition of cargo handling techniques.

In 1898, at a time when both models and toys had become more sought after and were more sophisticated in finish, thanks to the great strides made in engineering expertise during the Victorian era, the firm of Bassett-Lowke was founded in Northampton, a market town some 100 miles north of London. It sprang from another enterprise, JT Lowke & Sons, which made a speciality of castings and steam fittings for model-makers. The new firm concentrated at first on making models of railway locomotives, rolling stock and boiler fittings but within a few years, it also started to manufacture ship models. This activity was carried out at its nearby Winteringham works, which was gradually expanded to enable production of both simple working models as well as high-class scale exhibition models. Mr Wenman J Bassett-Lowke, the Managing Director, (although very much a 'railways man'), always showed a keen interest in the marine side of his company. It was his enthusiasm which encouraged the subsequent expansion of the firm's activities into the field which is the subject of this book.

Waterline models have a great advantage over full-hull models, in that they give the impression of a ship floating in its natural element. This is achieved by omitting the underwater part of the ship during construction from a point equivalent to where the water level would reach if the vessel were floating at her normal trim. As few people see ships out of the water (even in drydock),

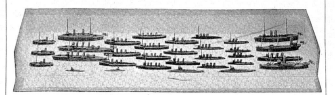

The BRITISH NAVY in Miniature.

Illustration of Set No. 153.   Price 4/6 per set.

During the early stages of the war the Commercial Intelligence Branch of the British Board of Trade organized a series of exhibitions of German-made toys, and showed great enterprise and courtesy in assisting English makers to take up the manufacture of toys hitherto exclusively made in Germany. We tender to them our thanks and appreciation for their efforts, and trust that every Briton will purchase only British goods when possible.

We had for many years past been manufacturing on a large scale every variety of Railway and Ship model, true to scale and possessing the characteristics of the original. We now offer to the public a comprehensive range of warship models, including practically every vessel in the British Navy, at an exceedingly low price, and claim this to be one of the first serious attempts to capture a little of the German toy trade as a result of the Board of Trade efforts.

The expense of making all the special dies and tools is very considerable, but we trust our numerous patrons and friends will support our new venture as generously as in the past. For our part we can conscientiously state these new models are splendid value for money, and cannot be surpassed for excellence of workmanship and finish.

The boats are finished in correct colours, and are all made to one uniform scale of 150 feet equals one inch, or one-eighteen-hundredth full size.

Practically every ship in the Navy has been modelled and every class of warship is available, including Super-Dreadnoughts, Battleships, Battle Cruisers, Armoured Cruisers, Light Cruisers, Destroyers, Torpedo Boats, Submarines, Mine Layers, Mine Sweepers, Troopships, Transports, Armed Liners, and all Auxiliary Craft.

HOW TO COLLECT THE MODELS.

Buy a box full—any box will do as a start. Just a 1/6 box, and you will become a collector of naval models. You just can't help it! The little ships fascinate you so, you simply *must* have a fleet of your own. Their neat and businesslike appearance appeals irresistibly—and, after all, their cost is very, very little, while they teach you so much about the Navy, our gallant seamen, and their ships. Just suppose you bought Set No. 104, a cruiser squadron, as a start. With this one set of seven ships, costing 1/6, a number of manoeuvres can be carried out—but add Set No. 106, a destroyer flotilla, costing another 1/6, and see how much more interesting it is. Then a battleship squadron, say No. 136, priced at 3/-, and you can carry out naval actions such as those in the North Sea. While, if you want a Grand Fleet, buy Set No. 131, price 3/-, and so on, until you possess a complete set of models of every ship in the British Navy.

5

4. Extracts from a Bassett-Lowke WW1 (1914-1918) catalogue, which combined railways and ship models. This lists the pre-war range and offers some for sale during this wartime period. It provided the basis of the post-war 100ft.-1in. range of ship models.

it follows therefore that the majority only see ships afloat and it was this that led to the initial production and subsequent demand for waterline models.

The earliest waterline ship models made by Bassett-Lowke appeared at the turn of the century. They were constructed of wood and wire, were not to scale and were very basic and simple in finish. They were purely representative of a type or class of British warship.

All this changed around 1908, when Mr Edward Hobbs, a model boat enthusiast, joined Bassett-Lowke as the first manager of its London shop. It was he who arranged for a small independent company to produce miniature waterline models under sub-contract, with Bassett-Lowke taking responsibility for the marketing side. That small company was controlled by two gentlemen, a Mr Denton and a Mr Checker, who originally came from Czechoslovakia, and their products were made to a standard scale of 100 ft. to 1 in., or 1/1200th. This then was the first venture into the commercial field of selling small-scale handmade waterline model ships.

Initially only British Royal Navy vessels were available but later the range was extended to include warships of most nations. As the models were individually hand-crafted, they were naturally somewhat costly and consequently a selection of cheaper ship models, cast in

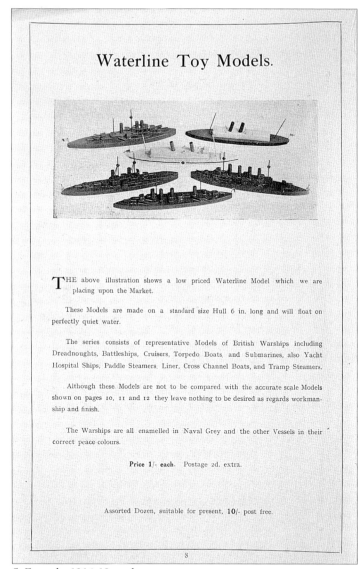

Waterline Toy Models.

THE above illustration shows a low priced Waterline Model which we are placing upon the Market.

These Models are made on a standard size Hull 6 in. long and will float on perfectly quiet water.

The series consists of representative Models of British Warships including Dreadnoughts, Battleships, Cruisers, Torpedo Boats, and Submarines, also Yacht Hospital Ships, Paddle Steamers, Liner, Cross Channel Boats, and Tramp Steamers.

Although these Models are not to be compared with the accurate scale Models shown on pages 10, 11 and 12 they leave nothing to be desired as regards workmanship and finish.

The Warships are all enamelled in Naval Grey and the other Vessels in their correct peace colours.

Price 1/- each. Postage 2d. extra.

Assorted Dozen, suitable for present, 10/- post free.

8

5. *From the 1914-18 catalogue.*

white metal, were produced to a smaller scale of 150 feet to 1 inch. An extract is included from a B-L catalogue produced during WW1, which lists these models together with the early 100 ft. to 1 in. ones. It is interesting to note that Bassett-Lowke was instructed by the government at that time, not to sell any Royal Navy ship models to the public and consequently they were not listed. Bassett-Lowke continued to produce and sell ship models in the smaller scales of 125 ft. to 1 in. and 150 ft. to 1 in. up to the 1920s, but these were only made in very limited numbers, covering just a narrow range of warships, and are outside the scope of this book.

The public appetite for waterline ship models had been whetted by an event that took place at London's Earls Court exhibition hall in 1913, namely the Imperial Services Exhibition. In honour of the occasion, Bassett-Lowke had been commissioned to produce a special display of 100 ft. to 1 in. warships of all nations to illustrate the comparative strengths of the different navies in relation to types and numbers of vessels. This attracted considerable public attention and really brought miniature waterline models into their own.

Over eighty years later, few of these early models are still in existence but it can be seen from those which do

6. A photograph of part of the display at the 1913 Imperial Services Exhibition.

7. Waterline naval models being assembled; at right: Mr Blank, 1920s.

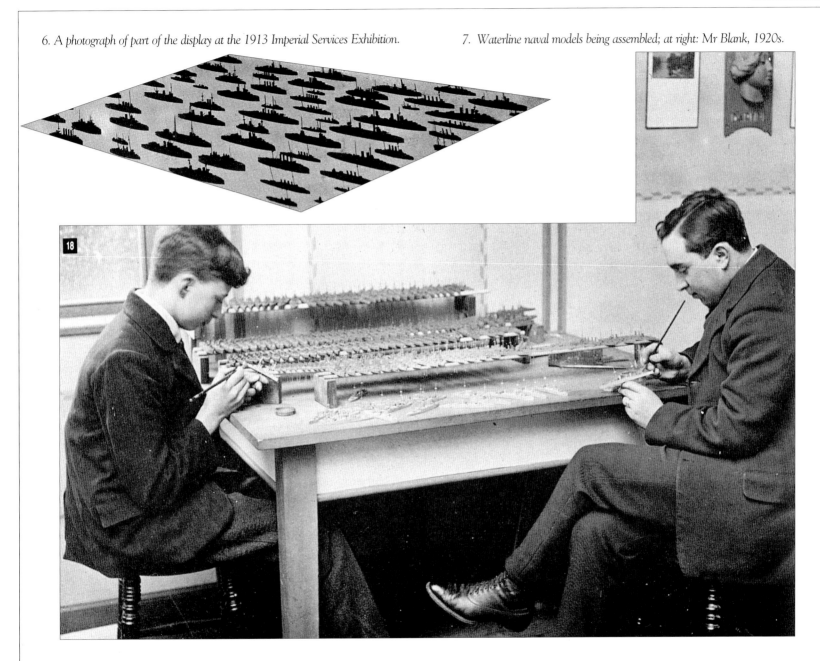

The Latest Topical Novelty.

IN addition to the boxed metal boats described in the preceding pages of this Catalogue which are produced entirely by machinery, we also make and supply hand-made waterline models built to a scale of **100 feet to the inch**. We can supply models of any type of battleship, cruiser, or any vessel of practically all the navies of the world. We have supplied many hundreds of these models for demonstration and other purposes.

Each ship is carefully and accurately made of selected wood, metal guns, and finished in proper naval colours.

The above illustration gives a good idea of a group of these models.

For Strategical Studies these little models are without comparison. Their accuracy enables various naval evolutions to be studied and carried out with ease, while the descriptions of fleet actions are simplified by using these models, placing them in the proper positions, and moving the models in accordance with the reported movements of the British and enemy vessels.

Another use for these models is that the profile of the ships can be studied, and the characteristics of various vessels learned, so that almost any different class of vessel may be recognised at a glance. For training for aerial observation these models are of incalculable value and interest.

The Lords Commissioners of the Admiralty have requested us to withdraw from sale during the period of the War waterline scale models of British Warships. These models, however, can still be supplied to members of H.M. Navy under certain conditions. The above regulations do not apply to models of British Merchant Ships, etc., or allied, neutral and belligerent warships, which can still be supplied to the public.

We have spared no pains to finish these models as accurately as the small scale and price allows.

8. From the 1914-18 catalogue.

survive, that they had both charm and character. They were instrumental in starting the enthusiasm for collecting small replicas of both warships and merchant ships and, apart from being either souvenirs or toys, they were also used by the Allied Armed services for recognition and training purposes in both world wars. Such was the demand between the two world wars for models of all types, ranging from railway items to engineering subjects and from shipping to architecture, that Bassett-Lowke was forced to sub-contract much of its work out to other specialist model-makers. This applied equally to small-scale ship models, which were independently produced by Waterline Models, still in the capable hands of Messrs. Denton and Checker, and situated in Kingswell Street, Northampton. In 1938, however, their company was merged with Ship Models Ltd, the shipping arm of Bassett-Lowke, in order to serve the large contracts then being placed by the British armed forces, particularly the Admiralty. Following the amalgamation, the two companies remained in their own premises until 1941 when the former Waterline Models finally joined Ship Models Ltd at the rear of Bassett-Lowke's headquarters in St Andrews Street. They stayed in this accomodation until 1953 when the workshops were moved back to Kingswell Steet.

The British Navy in Miniature.

All these models are made to scale, possess the chief characteristics of the originals, and by making a collection of different boxes of these models a complete set representative of every ship in the Navy can be obtained. Each set is neatly put up in a cardboard box, and contains different selections of vessels.

Set No. 102.

Set No. 101. Battle Fleet—Containing Battleship "Lord Nelson," Battle Cruiser "Invincible," Armoured Cruiser "Drake," one Submarine, one Destroyer, one Torpedo Boat, and one Mine Sweeper.
Price 1/6 per set. Postage 4d.

Set No. 102. Battle Fleet—Containing Battleship "King Edward VII.," Battle Cruiser "Lion," Armoured Cruiser "Devonshire," Submarine, Torpedo Boat, and two Destroyers. Price 1/6 per set. Postage 4d.

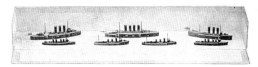

Set No. 104.

Set No. 103. Battle Fleet—Containing Super-Dreadnoughts "Orion," "Queen Elizabeth," Cruiser "Hawke," Torpedo Boat, Submarine, Destroyer, and Tug. Price 1/6 per set. Postage 4d.

Set No. 104. Cruiser Squadron—Containing Cruisers "Diadem," "Challenger," and "Kent," and four fast Torpedo Boat Destroyers.
Price 1/6 per set. Postage 4d.

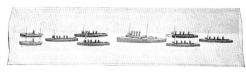

Set No. 106.

Set No. 105. Battleship Squadron—Containing Battleships "Swiftsure," "Canopus," "Majestic," one Submarine, one Torpedo Boat, and two Destroyers. Price 1/6 per set. Postage 4d.

Set No. 106. Destroyer Flotilla with Leader—Containing Light Cruiser "Undaunted," six Destroyers, two Mine Sweepers.
Price 1/6 per se. Postage 4d.

9. From the 1914-18 catalogue.

The British Navy in Miniature.

Set No. 107.

Set No. 107. Troopships with Convoy—Containing Troopships "Egypt" and "India," Cruiser "Hampshire," two Tugs, and two Submarines.
Price 1/6 per set. Postage 4d.

Set No. 108. Australian Navy—Containing Battle Cruiser "Australia," Light Cruisers "Melbourne" and "Sydney," three Torpedo Boats, and Destroyer "Paramatta." Price 1/6 per set. Postage 4d.

Set No. 109.

Set No. 109. Light Cruiser Patrol Squadron—Containing Light Cruisers "Arethusa" and "Aurora," six fast Destroyers, and Submarine.
Price 1/6 per set. Postage 4d.

Set No. 110. Hospital and Troopship with Convoy.—Containing one Hospital Ship, one Troopship, one Scout, two Mine Sweepers, and two Destroyers. Price 1/6 per set. Postage 4d.

Set No. 112.

Set No. 111. Dreadnought Squadron—Containing Super-Dreadnoughts "Iron Duke," "King George V.," the "Dreadnought," three Destroyers and one Submarine. Price 1/6 per set. Postage 4d.

Set No. 112. Spithead Review—Containing Royal Yacht "Victoria and Albert," Light Cruiser "Birmingham," escort of six Destroyers, and one Submarine. Price 1/6 per set. Postage 4d.

10. From the 1914-18 catalogue.

Prices of Scale Model Warships.

The above Illustration shows a representative set of the latest ships of the German Navy, also s.s. "Olympic" and s.s. "Imperator."

Each Model is packed in a separate box and enamelled in best style.

Torpedo Boats and Destroyers, about 2½ ins. long. French, Russian,
German, Austrian, Japanese, Italian, etc. ...
Submarines. French, Russian, German, Austrian, Japanese, Italian, etc. } 3/- each.
Mine Sweepers and Mine Layers ... ...

CRUISERS.

French—Condé, Victor Hugo, Jules Ferry, Ernest Renan, Edgar Quinet,
Waldeck Rousseau ...
German—Emden, Breslau, Stralsund, Strassburg, Magdeburg ...
U.S.A.—North Carolina, Montana, Washington, Tennessee ... } 6/- ,,
Austrian—Saida, Helgoland, Novara, Sankt Georg
Russian—Rurik, Admiral Makaroff, Bayan ...
Japanese—Nisshin, Kasuga ...

BATTLESHIPS.

French—Massina, Democratie, Justice, Verité ... ...
German—Deutschland, Hannover, Pommern, Schleswig-Holstein,
Schlesie
Austrian—Erzherzog Karl, Franz Ferdinand, Zrinzi, Radetzky ... } 6/6 ,,
Italian—Pisa, Amalfi, San Giorgio, San Marco ...
Russian—Imperator Paval, Andrei Pervosivami ... ...
U.S.A.—Kansas, Vermont, Minnesota, New Hampshire...
Japanese—Kastuma, Katori ...

DREADNOUGHTS, SUPER-DREADNOUGHTS & BATTLE CRUISERS.

French—Normandie, Gascoyne, Languedoc, Flandres, Bearn, Bretagne,
Lorraine, Provence, Courcet, Jean Bart, Paris, France, Danton,
Mirabeau, Diderot, Condorcet, Vergniand, Voltaire ...
German—Kronprinz, Grosse Kurfurst, Kœnig, Markgraf, Kaiser,
Freidrich der Grosse, Kaiserin, Prinz Regent Luitpold, Konig
Albert, Thuringen, Helgoland, Ostfriesland, Oldenburg, Derfflin- } 7/6 each.
ger, Lutzov, Ersatz Hertha, Seydlitz, Molke Goeben, Von der Tann
Austrian—Viribus Unibus, Tegetthof, P. Eugen, Szent Istrav ...
Italian—Conte di Cavour ...
Russian—Gangoot, Poltava, Petroparlovsk, Sevastopol, Imperator
Alexandre III. ... ...

The Torpedo Boat Destroyers are enamelled in black; Warships in the different naval colours; and the Liners in the colours of the respective companies.

Any Ship not mentioned in the above list can be made specially to order at 1/- extra on above prices.

10

11. From the 1914-18 catalogue.

Waterline Models of the Mercantile Marine of the World.

THE Success of our Waterline Models of Warships has induced us to place upon the Market a special series of similar Models of the Mercantile Marine made to the same scale, viz:—100 ft. to the 1 in.

The above illustration shows a selection of five of these Models, viz:— "Aquitania," "Olympic," "Lusitania," "Macedonia," and "Ville de Liege."

At the Scale of 100 ft. to the 1 in. some of the Ships are 9 or 10 in. long and range down to about 3 in. in the case of the Channel Packets. The adoption of a standard scale for these Models enables a comparison to be made of the size and general build of the Ships modelled. As much detail as is possible with the small scale is put into these miniature ships and all the leading features are accurately reproduced. Every Ship is enamelled in the standard peace colours of the respective Companies and a group of these Ships makes a very attractive display.

Prices and particulars are as follows:—
                                                    Prices, including Postage.
Cunard Liner, "Aquitania" (finished as Hospital Ship) 17/6
White Star Liner, "Olympic" or "Titanic" 15/6
Hamburg-American Liner, "Imperator" or "Vaterland" 15/6
Cunard Liner "Mauretania" or "Lusitania" ... 12/6
Compagnie General Transatlantique," France" 10/6
Allan Liner "Alsatian" 10/6
North German Lloyd Liner, "Kronprinzessin Cecilie" 10/6
Union Castle Liner "Balmoral Castle" 10/6
Hamburg-American Liner, "Cap Trafalgar" 10/6
Canadian Pacific Liner, "Empress of Asia" or "Empress of Russia" ... 10/6
Royal Mail Steam Packet, "Asturias" or "Amazon" 9/6
American Line Steamer, "St. Louis" or "St. Paul" 9/6
Orient Liner "Otranto" 8/6
P. & O. Liner, "Macedonia," etc. 8/6
Royal Holland Steamship Co.'s Steamer, "Gelria" or "Tubantia" ... 7/6
Booth Steamship Co.'s Steamer "Hilary" 6/6
Steam Yacht, "The Viking" 6/6
S. E. & C. Rly. Cross Channel Packet, "Engadine" or "Riviera" ... 5/6
Dover & Ostend Steamship Co.'s Steamer, "Ville de Liege" ... 5/6

EACH MODEL IS PACKED SEPARATELY IN A CARDBOARD BOX.

P.S.—We have other Models in course of preparation.

11

12. From the 1914-18 catalogue.

13-15. A selection of letters from Bassett-Lowke to the author over a thirty year period.

BASSETT-LOWKE LTD

MAKERS OF MODELS TO SCALE
18/25 KINGSWELL ST · NORTHAMPTON

TELEPHONE 4122 & 4123

OUR REF. HWF/AM. YOUR REF.

D. Head Esq.,   12th April 1955
12, Withdean Court,
Preston Park,
BRIGHTON.

Dear Sir,

In answer to your letter of the 6th, due to
extreme pressure of work, and other difficulties it
has not been possible to re-develop our range of
100'-1" scale Waterline models such as we offered
in pre-war days.

However, we have three available from stock at
the moment all at £10 10s. complete in perspex case,
the price includes the Purchase Tax post free to your
address. The vessels concerned are the three liners:-

Queen "Elizabeth",
the "Mauretania",
and the "Corona".

Yours faithfully,

BASSETT-LOWKE LTD.,

LONDON BRANCH: 112 HIGH HOLBORN · W·C·1   MANCHESTER BRANCH: 28 CORPOR
TELEPHONE: HOLBORN 6285

BASSETT-LOWKE LTD

MAKERS OF MODELS TO SCALE
18/25 KINGSWELL ST · NORTHAMPTON

TELEPHONE 4122 & 4123

OUR REF. RHF/AMV   YOUR REF.
H85

13th July, 1962.

Derek Head Esq., V.R.D., A.R.I.B.A.,

Dear Sir,

We thank you for your letter of the 12th
July, and would state that the cost of making to
special order a model of the Shaw Savill "NORTHERN STAR"
to a scale of 100'0" to 1" would be in the region of
£25 0s.0d.

Yours faithfully,

BASSETT-LOWKE LTD.

LONDON BRANCH: 112 HIGH HOLBORN · W·C·1   MANCHESTER BRANCH: 28 CORPORATIO
TELEPHONE: HOLBORN 6285   TELEPHONE: BLACKFRIARS 0229

18th August 1987

Bassett-Lowke (SM) Ltd.
Harvey Reeves Road
Northampton NN5 5JR
Tel: (0604) 585999

Our ref:MF/FH

BASSETT LOWKE

Directors:
A. P. RITCHIE B.Sc. (Chairman)
M. FIELDING C.Eng. M.I.Mech.E. M.I.E.D.
R. R. RITCHIE C.Eng. M.I.Mech.E. M.I.Prod.E.
D. J. SENTER A.C.A. (Secretary)

D.Head Esq.,

Dear Derek,

Following our recent telephone conversations regarding
Bassett-Lowke Water-Line models it would appear that the
production runs were as follows:

For any class of ship 1-200 off, but for the Great Ocean
Liners (i.e. Normandie) 1000 off were made.

You will appreciate that these figures are based on memory
only, there being no production records available.

I trust this will be of assistance.

With kind regards.

Yours sincerely,

M.Fielding
Director

Regd. in England No. 246510 at
Dunraven Street Industrial Estate
Bridgend CF31 3UF

⟫ WARSHIP MODELS ⟪

In 1911 the British Admiralty placed an order with Bassett-Lowke for the supply of a substantial number of 100 ft. to 1 in. waterline ship models, which were to be used as teaching aids for the Royal Navy. As ships of that period were relatively basic in design and layout – comprising hulls, funnels, masts and guns – so were the models. They were, however, fundamentally correct in scale and limited detail. Production of these models continued until 1919 and during those eight years, several thousand were made, although, sadly, few have survived to the present day.

In the ensuing peace the only warship models produced by Bassett-Lowke, with one exception, were of British warships – 'the odd man out' being the German 'pocket' battleship ERSATZ PRUSSEN, later renamed DEUTSCHLAND. The range of warship models on offer was very limited, however, compared to the list of merchant ships. This is clearly illustrated in the reproduction of a page from the B-L catalogue issued in November 1933.

All the warship models produced in the 1920s and 1930s for sale to the general public were constructed from information available in the well-known publication Jane's Fighting Ships – an annual which listed and illustrated, by photograph and plan, most of the major ships in the world's navies. However, whether intentionally or otherwise, the drawings of British warships were frequently inaccurate in hull form, profile and superstructure detail. As a result the models were also incorrect. They were, though, sufficiently accurate to enable the type or class of ship to be readily recognizable. This rather strange quirk can be easily illustrated by comparing these commercial models with those made for the Navy and RAF during WW2.

17. A late 19th century photograph illustrating the use of a ship model to teach sails and rigging to sailors of the Victorian navy. The part-model in the right of the photograph was used for demonstrating anchors and cable work.

The recognition models made for the Royal Navy and the RAF between 1936 and 1950 were to dramatically change this state of affairs. The design of warships had by then become far more complicated, both in main armament, secondary weapons systems, greatly enlarged superstructures, deck layout and hull form. All these changes had to be incorporated in the models, which were constructed with the use of official plans and photographs.

In 1936 Bassett-Lowke was commissioned by the Admiralty to make four sample models of HM Ships NELSON, FURIOUS, RENOWN and LEANDER – a battle-

ship, an aircraft carrier, a battle-cruiser and a cruiser respectively. A photograph of these models is illustrated in an extract from the 1936 Bassett-Lowke catalogue (page 64) and comparison can be made with the battle-cruiser's sister ship REPULSE as shown in the 1933 edition. After assessing their value for teaching identification and other training purposes, the Royal Navy, followed shortly afterwards by the RAF, ordered similar models in large numbers for issue to service establishments, naval bases and airfields. The quality, finish and detailing of these Bassett-Lowke models was quite superb, far surpassing any produced hitherto. Their hulls were carved out of a suitable hardwood, with Bristol board being employed for the decks, wire for the masts and guns, and paper for the funnels, though sometimes more complex ones such as the BISMARK's, would be turned in brass.

These recognition models were usually to be found in information or intelligence rooms, where they were displayed either on table tops or on shelves. Sometimes as I found, in one shore establishment, the models were securely locked away in a cabinet and considerable persuasion was required to get them produced. The reason for this precaution was probably that, being chargeable store items – not cheap even at that period, those responsible for their safe-keeping had to account for them at each 'muster'. On a later occasion, I discovered that a 100 ft. to 1 in. model of the aircraft carrier ARK ROYAL, incidentally not made by Bassett-Lowke, was listed in 1980 in naval stores as being valued at £88. This was one of the very few survivors of the post-war recognition models made for the Ministry of Defence, most probably by the official Admiralty model-maker, Julian Glossop, or his son.

18. A forecastle model, c.1950, to teach anchor and cable work to cadets at Britannia Royal Naval College, Dartmouth.

19. Far left: Another illustration of a bow section of a warship used for instruction.

20. Left: Pre-war naval cadets using a model of HMS NELSON/RODNEY for instructional purposes. The considerable size of these teaching models enabled extensive detail to be included, some of which was made to work mechanically.

In HMS DOLPHIN, the submarine base at Gosport, Bassett-Lowke models in both 100 feet and 50 feet to the inch were successfully used in the submarine 'attack-teacher', a device used to train prospective submarine officers. The models mainly came into their own, however, when they were on permanent display, grouped in their respective scales, for then their three-dimensional characteristics and in particular the contrast in size between different types, for they were all to the same scale, could be fully studied and appreciated.

An enquiry made some years ago to Bassett-Lowke, to try to establish the scope of their wartime production of waterline warship models, prompted the reply that if one consulted *Jane's Fighting Ships* for that period, then most of the ships illustrated had been made by the company. On reflection, I think that this claim was reasonably justified. As evidence I have in my own collection some 212 examples of different warships, all made by Bassett-Lowke between 1938 and 1952, and these range from an unlikely model of the Italian cruiser BARI (1935) to HM Submarine ALCIDE (1950). This number does not include models of ships which were frequently re-issued, in order to incorporate the many modifications made during the course of the war. Unlike the

21. *Submariners under instruction at HMS DOLPHIN, the submarine base at Gosport, Hampshire with the 'Attack Teacher', and using a 1/600 scale model of the Russian cruiser MAXIM GORKI.*
(Reproduced by kind permission of the Royal Navy Submarine Museum).

22. *Officers at HMS DOLPHIN undergoing ship recognition training early in the 1939/45 war with 1/600 scale models. Those being used are the BREMEN/ EUROPA, the CAVOUR, FIJI, the LITTORIO being held, the KING GEORGE V, NEW ORLEANS, the German passenger/cargo ship REICHENFELS and the Italian cruiser GARIBALDI in the foreground.*
(Reproduced by kind permission of the Royal Navy Submarine Museum Gosport).

23. *Early Bassett-Lowke 1/1200 warship models, circa 1914-1922, with the contemporary boxes. The models represent HMS CANOPUS, HMS VINDICTIVE, HMS MAJESTIC, HMS TIGER, HMS HOOD, USN CALIFORNIA, IDAHO and NEVADA, IJS FUSO, ISE and KUMA and the GMS VON-DER-TANN in the foreground. These models are all from the Randolph Poulos collection.*

Great War of 1914-1918, technical advancements and lessons learnt in battle caused changes to be made to most warships between 1939 and 1946. I have no less than three Bassett-Lowke models of the cruiser HMS ARETHUSA, each of which is different in detail. They show her at separate stages in her wartime career. The first is prior to her refitting with four twin 4" anti-aircraft guns; the second as modified with the new armament and with tripod masts, as at April 1942; and the third, dated April 1944, shows the ship after a further refit and minus her centre-line crane.

Another example of different models being issued for the same vessel, as a result of alteration, is HMS RENOWN, where one model covers her wartime guise and another is dated 20th May 1947. Both of them are excellent in terms of quality and finish.

Some representative models are in very short supply, especially those of ships which had only a short life. I was fortunate enough to obtain a 1940 model of the aircraft carrier HMS GLORIOUS from a model-maker who worked at Bassett-Lowke both before and during the last war. The company had produced only a few of these models when, in August 1940, GLORIOUS was sunk and the Admiralty apparently had no further use for them. This resulted in the very limited number finding homes elsewhere.

In the Royal Navy these recognition aids were supplied to all training establishments and tactical schools, to Fleet Air Arm stations, certain specialised departments, including those dealing with ship camouflage, and to most capital ships such as battleships and fleet aircraft carriers. The RAF appears to have issued them to all Coastal Command airfields, some Bomber Command stations and also to certain Fighter Command bases, both in the UK and overseas. In addition Bassett-Lowke also supplied many 50ft. to 1in. ship models to both services, as this was the other scale used for recognition and training purposes. Many of these larger models included ship's boats, which were generally omitted on their smaller sisters, though by no means all of them, as can be seen from the illustrations of some of my own models.

For some reason that is beyond me, Bassett-Lowke painted their warship models in different shades of grey depending on which nation they belonged to. For instance, Royal Navy ships were light grey, tinged with blue and, I suspect, a touch of yellow. US ones were mid-grey, Italian ones slightly darker, whilst those of Germany and Japan were painted a very dark grey. These colours bore no relation to the actual colours used on the full-size ships, but knowledge of this colouring system often helped students to identify the nationality of a vessel merely by its shade of grey, although this was not the object of the exercise. However, this was dependent on their ability to first recognise that the model had in fact been made by Bassett-Lowke, as other manufacturers were inconsistent in their painting techniques. On a final painting note, the last Bassett-Lowke recognition models produced for the Royal Navy in 1952 were of the Russian cruisers CHAPAEV and MAXIM GORKI, both finished in a strange green colour!

The Royal Navy numbered the models made for it, both in the 50ft. to 1in. and 100ft. to 1in. scales, firstly with a letter denoting the country of origin, then a number identifying the ship or class of ship, followed by an additional letter L or S referring to the larger or smaller scales respectively. The final letters were often omitted from the label placed under the model, or on its box, where the scale was already shown. Examples of the labelling system are:– B19 for HMS ARETHUSA; A7 USS SOUTH DAKOTA; F18 JEAN BART (France); I14 BALENO (Italy); and J12 ZINTU (Japan).

The RAF, which also made use of both scales, employed a different system. It numbered all models

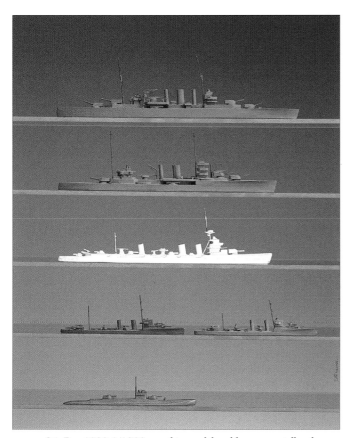

*24. Pre-1939 1/1200 warship models sold commercially: the
LONDON, YORK, ENTERPRISE, 'B' Class destroyer,
KEMPENFELT and Submarine 'X1'. Some of these models have
been repainted and form part of a collection of over 180
Bassett-Lowke warship models, all labelled, acquired in 1992
by David Hughes of London.*

*25. Further models from David Hughes' collection of the FURIOUS, REPULSE,
QUEEN ELIZABETH, ROYAL SOVEREIGN and HAWKINS. All these British war-
ship models typify those marketed by Bassett-Lowke between the two World
Wars and it is likely that many were made for a special order around 1935-
1936. Most of Mr Hughes' acquisitions are of warship models not listed by
Bassett-Lowke covering American, German, Japanese and French ships.
Again most of these models have been repainted at some time in the past.*

with a prefix of 52/ followed by the ship number and no nationality letter. Thus the destroyer HMS ESKIMO was listed as 52/125; the US cruiser AUGUSTA as 52/142; the French carrier BEARN as 52/173; and the Japanese cruiser NATORI as 52/166.

Sometimes the letter X can be found after the number on the RN models, denoting that a revision has been made to that particular class of warship. An example of this is HMS GLASGOW – a 'Southampton' class cruiser. I have three models of this ship, each one different. The first shows her in her original guise as at 1938, the second shows her fitted with additional gunnery director control towers after 1940 and the third following a later refit, which saw the removal of 'X' turret aft.

The numbering for the first two models is identical but has been changed to B16X for the last one (see page 35).

In 1939, when the war clouds were gathering over Europe once again, Mr Fuller, the manager of Bassett-Lowke's London shop in High Holborn, was told to take various measures to meet the greatly increasing number of orders. This included a new workshop in the basement and the training of two assistants.

Once the war had begun, the Bassett-Lowke workshops in Northampton and the satellite one in London found themselves unable to cope with the tremendous demand from the forces for small-scale model ships and were forced to look elsewhere for assistance. One offer of help came from a Miss Judith Hughes, who lived and worked in Devon. She was well suited to the task as she had her own cabinet-making business and Mr Bassett-Lowke lost no time in taking her on as a sub-contractor. Between the fall of France in 1940 and 1946, Miss Hughes and her assistants turned out over a thousand ship models in the 100ft. to 1in. scale for both the Royal Navy and the Royal Air Force. They all went under the Bassett-Lowke label and the quality of her workmanship certainly equalled in every respect that perfected by Bassett-Lowke in Northampton.

Fortunately for us Miss Hughes kept all her records,

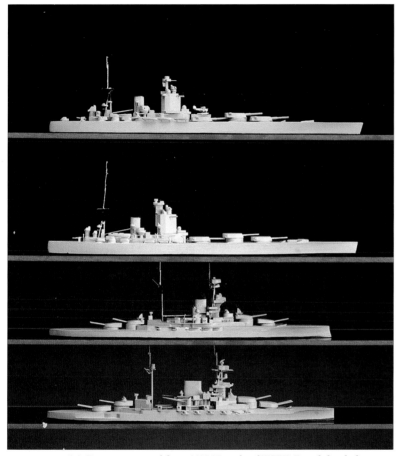

26. Recognition models to 1/1200 scale of WW2 British battleships: RODNEY, NELSON, ROYAL SOVEREIGN and MALAYA. These models were issued 1942/1943.

27. Far left. A close-up of the 1/1200 scale model of RODNEY, with an aircraft on the catapult forward of the bridge.

(see Appendix II), relating to the models made for Bassett-Lowke and these give the names of the ships and the month and year of manufacture. They make fascinating reading and cover an extensive range of some ninety different classes of vessel, from all types of warships to different merchant vessels, including both the Cunard 'Queens'. Miss Hughes continued to supply models to Bassett-Lowke after the war and these included the liners ILE DE FRANCE and ORCADES.

During the war, suitable timber for model making was often difficult to come by and seasoned lime, the wood normally used by Bassett-Lowke, virtually impossible to obtain. However the company managed to solve the problem in a rather novel way. It found that the fruit crates that arrived in the UK from America were made of a wood that was ideal for model making: close-grained, seasoned and hard enough to provide a crisp finish. It was never discovered exactly what these fruit crates were made of, but it was christened 'fruit wood' and this salvaged material served the company's needs well throughout the war years.

In 1946 production of recognition models was dramatically reduced following the termination of hostilities and many of those held by both services were released for sale to the public. Other models also found their way, by devious means, into shops or collectors'

28. Bow view of HMS QUEEN ELIZABETH to 1/1200 scale.

hands. As their value as recognition aids diminished in the post-war years, due to the advent of more sophisticated methods of teaching, so their importance waned and many of the models were often considered to be expendable.

In October 1985 the final batches of British Ministry of Defence 100ft. to 1in. ship models were publicly auctioned off at Southampton and Exeter as Government surplus stores. There were 120 in all covering 25 different classes of warships and I was delighted to find amongst them a Bassett-Lowke model of the USS BALTIMORE, a heavy cruiser, dated June 1948.

Looking back, it is a good reflection on the quality of both modellers and materials that after, in most cases, more than fifty years, these B-L models are still in prime and stable condition. The same cannot be said of some other materials, such as the early plastics, where models suffered not only from 'lead disease' with its resultant deterioration, but also from some components degenerating into a form of ascetic acid, which led to a model assuming the shape of a banana! No such thing ever happened to a Bassett-Lowke model.

At the end of WW2, Rear Admiral Lyster, Royal Navy, who was then 5th Sea Lord and Chief of the Naval Air service, wrote to Bassett-Lowke with the following tribute:

"...I wonder if those who make these models really understand the great part their models play in the training of the Royal Navy in their work at sea.

"Ship recognition plays such a vital part in all sea warfare and as far as my own branch of the service is concerned, that is the Fleet Air Arm, an early appreciation by the aircrews and recognition of what they see during their reconnaissance flights over the ocean is invaluable and I do not think we should be able to reach the high state of training which we get, without the assistance of Bassett-Lowke models."

This well-earned praise should give additional plea-

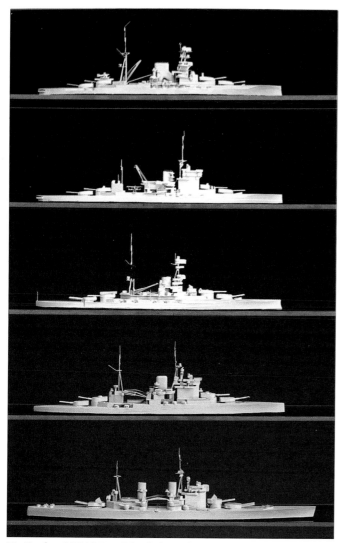

sure to the collector. He or she can appreciate their quality and workmanship, but also take pride in the knowledge that these particular 'works of art' have served an invaluable role in the conduct of a world war and have survived to become part of history. Not only do they provide a three-dimensional reminder of the majority of warships active during World War 2, but they also reproduce very accurately in miniature, the design, layout and fighting qualities of the ships of that period.

Fortunately, many of these models are still in existence and can be found at auctions, 'swop-meets' and

29. *Further 1/1200 British battleships of similar period to No.12: including* BARHAM, WARSPITE, RESOLUTION, QUEEN ELIZABETH *(1944) and* KING GEORGE V.

30. *HMS* KING GEORGE V, *1/1200.*

even some antique shops. It is up to collectors to find, preserve and value them, for it is certain that never again will craftsmen mass produce such individually handmade objects to the standard of perfection that

was achieved during the years of the 1940s.

In my own collection, I now have some 260 WW2 examples of Bassett-Lowke warships, representing the navies of Great Britain and the Commonwealth, the

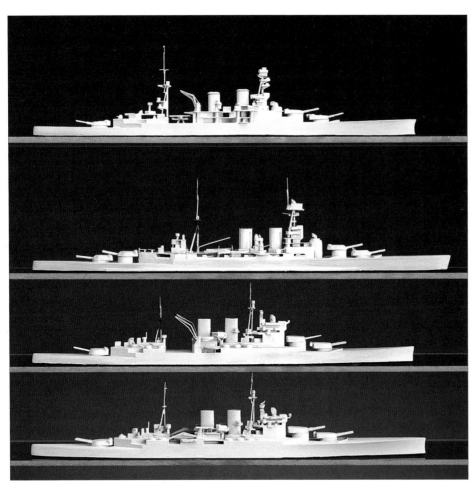

31. British Battle cruisers to 1/1200 scale: REPULSE, HOOD, RENOWN (1942) and RENOWN as refitted dated 20/5/47. The last recognition model was one of the few made by Bassett-Lowke after the war ended.

USA, France, the Netherlands, Germany, Italy, Japan and Russia.

After 1946, Bassett-Lowke re-entered the commercial world with the sale of a limited number of warship models. These are shown in the illustrated extract from a small catalogue issued in 1948 but the supply of these models only lasted a couple of years before being discontinued. I was astonished to discover, when purchas-

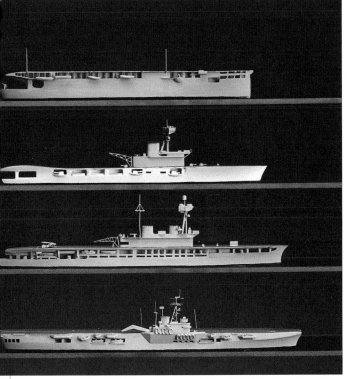

32. 1/1200 recognition models of British aircraft carriers: ARGUS, HERMES, EAGLE and GLORY.

33. Further 1/1200 British carriers: GLORIOUS, FURIOUS (1938), FURIOUS (1941) and ARK ROYAL. The 1938 FURIOUS must be one of the very few pre-war (1939) B-L recognition models made for the Admiralty to survive to the present day.

ing a model of HMS KING GEORGE V in 1949, that it was incorrect. I can only assume that, as Bassett-Lowke must have had the official plans of the ship for their war-time work, they had not been allowed to use them commercially and consequently the errors were intentional. The company never admitted to this charge, but as I did not buy any other warship models listed in their post-war catalogue, I cannot comment on them. Instead I turned to the war-time recognition ones as these I know to be accurate and very collectable.

34. *The after part of the flight deck of HMS ILLUSTRIOUS to 1/1200 scale.*

I have, in the main, concentrated on the 100ft. to 1in. models but examples do survive of Bassett-Lowke's larger 50ft. to 1in. warship and merchant vessel range. The quality of these is just as good as their smaller sisters but their greater size allowed the inclusion of more detail if required. However the number and type of ships covered was nothing like as extensive as in the 1/1200 range and due to their greater size they had less appeal for the collector, who was faced with storage and display problems. In addition, they did not correspond to any continental scale in the same way that the 1/1200 ones closely resembled the 1/1250 scale used by the Germans and other European manufacturers.

I have illustrated one typical display case of 50ft. to 1in. models of HM ships ILLUSTRIOUS (aircraft carrier), KING GEORGE V (battleship), UGANDA (cruiser) and JAVELIN (desroyer). These Bassett-Lowke models, packaged in a glass case, were issued to many RN shore establishments as well as to the Admiralty. I saw examples at HMS ROYAL ARTHUR, Skegness in 1942; HMS GLENDOWER, Pwllheli, Wales also in 1942; HMS HERON, RNAS Yeovilton in 1943 and in the Naval Intelligence Division of the Admiralty in London in 1944. All were identical save that HMS NIGERIA, a four-turret cruiser, was sometimes substituted for HMS UGANDA. A photograph of this display also appeared in

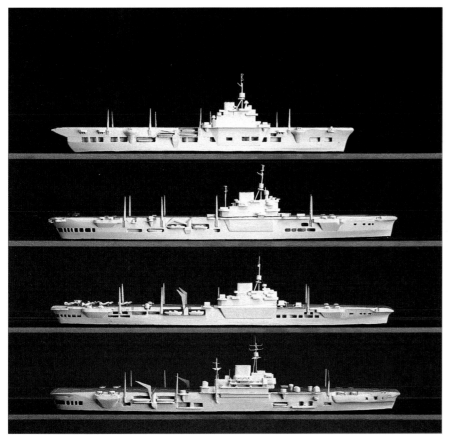

35. *The last of the 1/1200 British aircraft carrier recognition models:* UNICORN, INDOMITABLE, ILLUSTRIOUS *and* IMPLACABLE. *It will be noted that* INDOMITABLE *is different from those ships of the* ILLUSTRIOUS *class and this is the only model of this ship that I have seen. It is interesting that a model was commissioned, as she is so similar to her three earlier sisters in appearance.*

the Bassett-Lowke post-war model ship catalogue.

Other war-time manufacturers of miniature waterline recognition models included such firms as Sinclair Model Engineering Co., Glasgow; IR Amis Ltd., and Rowley Workshops Ltd., both of London; JJ and AT Bradford Ltd; Palatial Manufacturing Co. Ltd., Epsom; AD Services Ltd; Stewart Reidparth Ltd., Herne Bay, Philip Watson; E Mathews, Villeparle, Bombay, India; and, immediately after the last war, Commander M Norman RN of Parkham, Bideford.

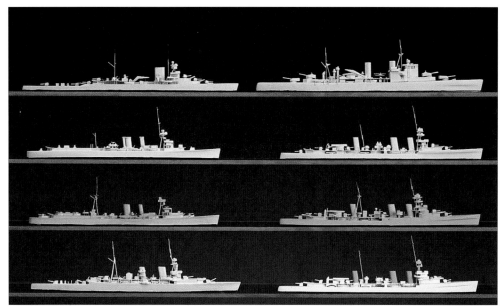

36. *1/1200 recognition models of British cruisers:* EFFINGHAM, LONDON, ADVENTURE *(1939),* EMERALD *(1939),* ADVENTURE *(1941),* EMERALD *(1942),* HAWKINS *and* EMERALD *in pre-war East Indies livery. This picture illustrates how models were re-issued after a ship's modification, with such alterations as tripod masts.*

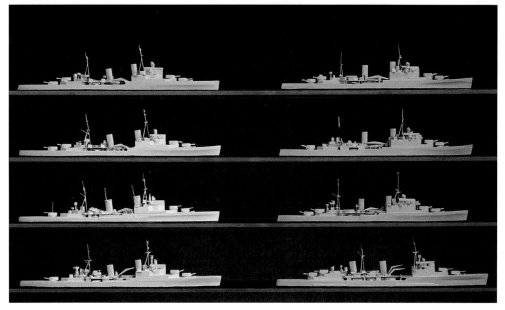

37. *1/1200 recognition models of three* COLONY *class cruisers: the* FIJI, UGANDA *and* BERMUDA, *and the* BELFAST.

40. The three SOUTHAMPTON class cruisers referred to on page 26, showing the GLASGOW (1938), the same ship in 1940 and finally after the removal of 'X' turret in 1945.

38. Heavy cruisers 1/1200: DEVONSHIRE, CORNWALL, DORSETSHIRE, EXETER (1941), YORK, EXETER (1938), KENT (1941), and KENT (1939).

39. Close-up of 1/1200 scale HMS NORFOLK in East Indies livery – she served on this station from 1935 to 1939.

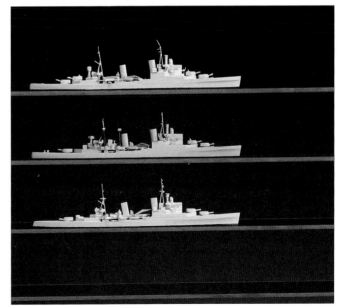

41. British light cruisers to 1/1200 scale: DAUNTLESS, DELHI (prior to refit), ORION, NEPTUNE, LEANDER (1946) and AMPHION.

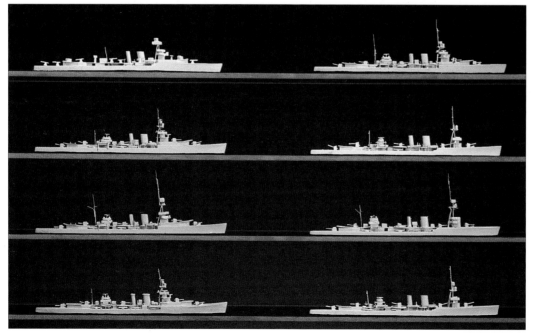

42. Further British light cruisers: the COVENTRY (as an AA cruiser), CURAÇOA, CAPETOWN, CALEDON, CARLISLE, CARADOC, COLOMBO and CALYPSO.

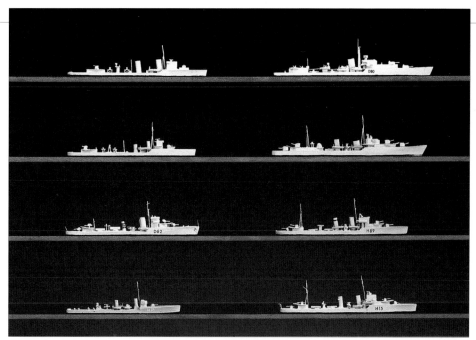

43. British 1/1200 destroyers: the WALLACE, BARFLEUR, WAIRS, AFRIDI, WILD SWAN, GRAFTON, SABRE and ECLIPSE.

44. British destroyers: CAVALIER, JANUS, TEAZER, JAVELIN, TYRION, MILNE, SOUTHDOWN and BEALSDALE.

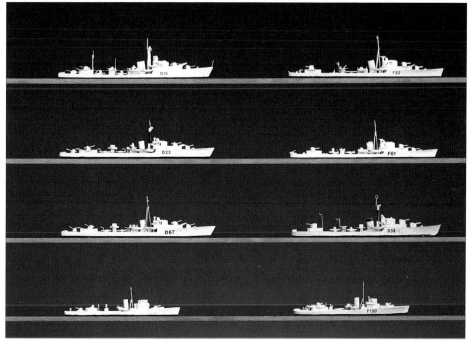

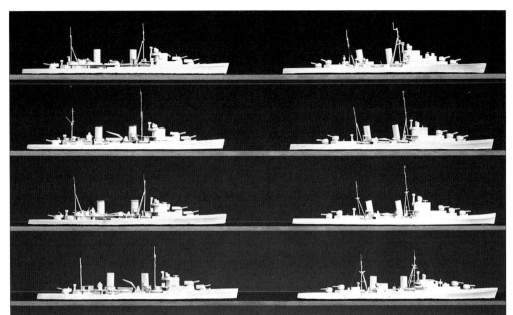

45. British cruisers at 1/1200 scale: ARETHUSA (1942), SIRIUS, ARETHUSA (1939), DIDO, ARETHUSA (1944), EURYALUS, GALATEA and DIADEM.

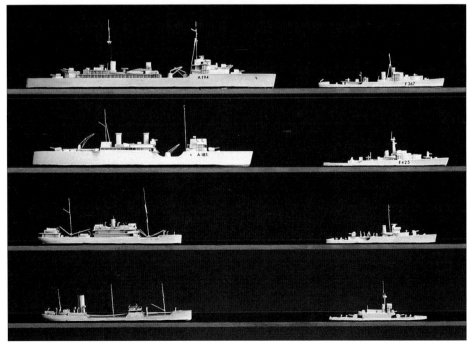

46. 1/1200 recognition models of British auxiliary support vessels and minor warships, the TYNE, TAFF, MAIDSTONE, LOCH DUNREGAN, TITANIA, LEITH, PETROLEUM and APHIS.

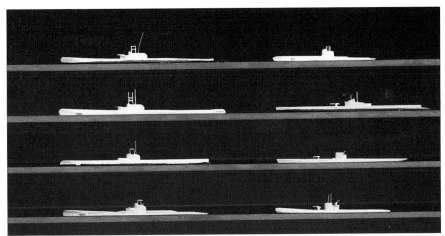

47. 1/1200 scale recognition model submarines: CLYDE, SWORDFISH, SEVERN, REDOUBTABLE and CACHELOT.

48. A war-time label affixed to the underside of a 1/1200 recognition model. These were utility labels, much smaller and narrower than those used pre-war and sometimes the ship's reference number was written on the label.

49. Left. Recognition models, scale 1/1200, of USA battleships: SOUTH DAKOTA, TENNESSEE (10/44), WASHINGTON, TENNESSEE (1940), ALASKA, WEST VIRGINIA, IOWA and MARYLAND (1944).

50. USA 1/1200 battleships: the MISSISSIPPI, NEW MEXICO, MARYLAND, NEVADA, COLORADO, PENNSYLVANIA, IDAHO and ARIZONA.

51. 1/1200 recognition models of aircraft carriers of the USA: the BOGUE, CASABLANCA, SANGAMON, INDEPENDENCE and RANGER.

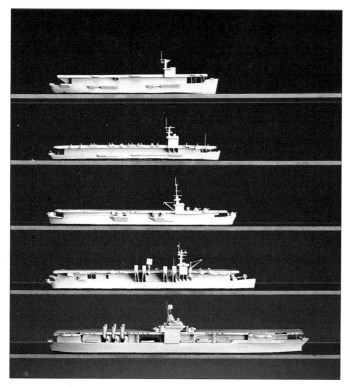

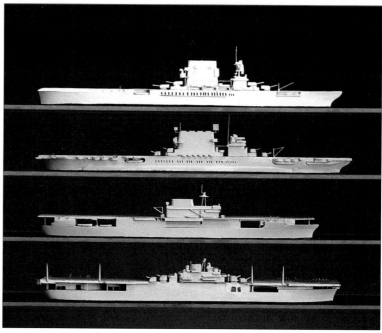

52. Further American carriers: LEXINGTON (1938), SARATOGA (1942), YORKTOWN and ESSEX.

53. Recognition models, scale 1/1200, of USA cruisers: the PENSACOLA, CHESTER, PENSACOLA (1939), PENSACOLA (1944), OMAHA and SALT LAKE CITY.

54. Further American cruisers: the PORTLAND, BROOKLYN, LOUISVILLE (1945), NEW ORLEANS, AUGUSTA and INDIANAPOLIS (1938).

55. Additional cruisers of the USA: WICHITA, BALTIMORE, PHILADELPHIA, CLEVELAND, ST LOUIS and ATLANTA.

56. Recognition models, to 1/1200 scale of auxiliaries and destroyers of the USA: DIXIE, CRANE, TERROR, FARRAGUT, MAURY and FLETCHER.

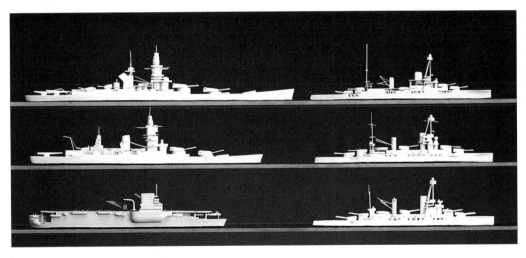

57. Recognition models of French battleships to 1/1200 scale: RICHELIEU, COUBERT, DUNKERQUE, PROVENCE, the aircraft carrier BEARN and the BRETAGNE.

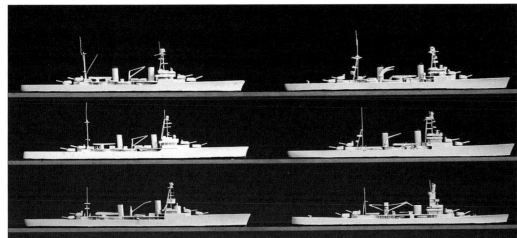

58. *1/1200 scale French cruisers:*
TOURVILLE, DUPLEIX, DUQUESNE, FOCH,
SUFFREN *and* ALGERIE.

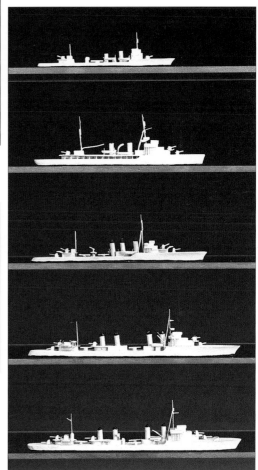

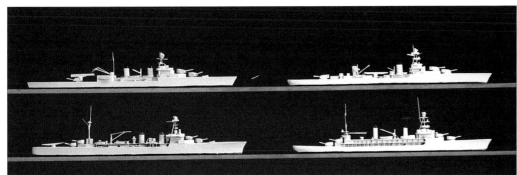

59. *Further 1/1200 scale French cruisers:*
the LA GALISSONNIERE, EMILE BERTIN,
DUGUAY TROUIN *and the* JEANNE D'ARC.

60. *French destroyers*
and a sloop: BRANLEBAS,
D'ENTRECASTEAUX,
L'ALCYON, GUEPARD
and AIGLE.

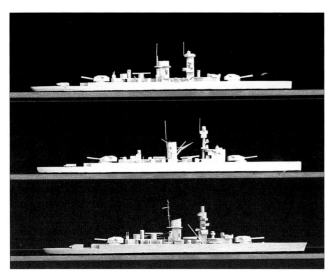

61. 1/1200 scale recognition models of the German pocket battleships GRAF SPEE, DEUTSCHLAND and ADMIRAL SCHEER.

63. Below. German battleships to 1/1200 scale: the SCHARNHORST, BISMARK, TIRPITZ and GNEISENAU.

1/1200 scale

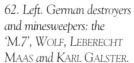

62. Left. German destroyers and minesweepers: the 'M.7', WOLF, LEBERECHT MAAS and KARL GALSTER.

64. Below. German cruisers: the PRINZ EUGEN, EMDEN, KOLN, ADMIRAL HIPPER, NURNBERG and LEIPZIG.

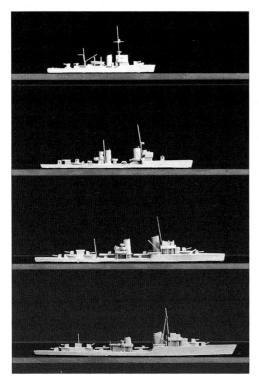

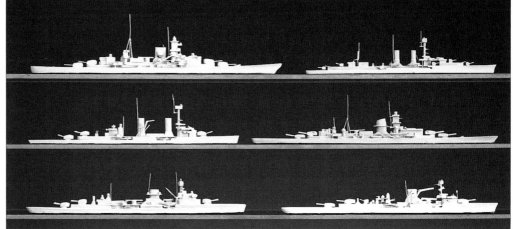

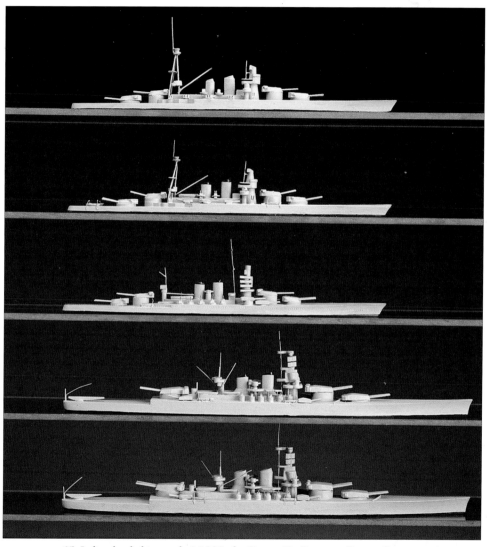

65. Italian battleships, scale 1/1200: the CONTE DI CAVOUR, GUILIO CESARE, ANDREA DORIA, *and the* LITTORIO.

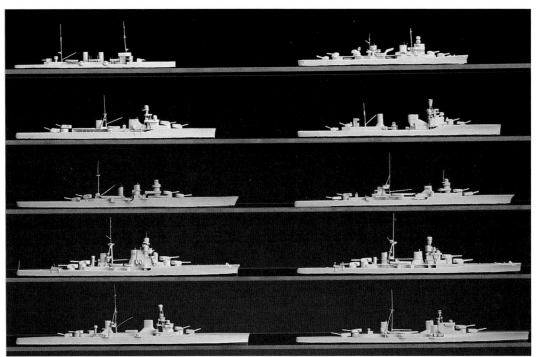

66. *1/1200 scale recognition models of Italian cruisers: the* BARI, ATTILIO REGOLO, LUIGI CARDONA, ALBERTO DI GIUSSANO, GUISEPPI GARIBALDI, TRENTO, POLA, ZARA, MONTECUCCOLI *and* BOLZANO.

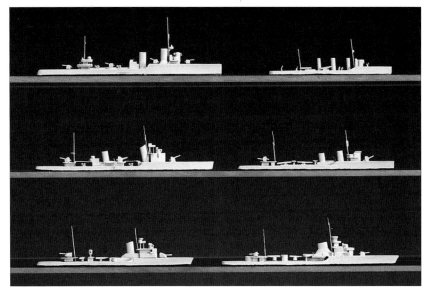

67. *Italian destroyers to 1/1200 scale:* LEONE, SIRTORI, LUCA TARIGO, BOREA, BALENO *and* GRECALE.

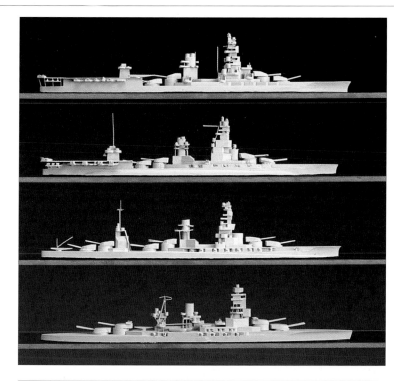

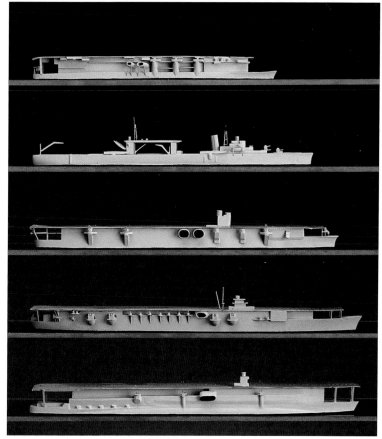

Japanese models to 1/1200 scale.

68. Left. Japanese battleships Ise (1945), Hyuga (1945), Hyuga (1942), and Nagato.

69. Japanese aircraft carriers Ryuzyo, Chitose, Soru, Shokaku and Kaga.

70. Left. Recognition models, scale 1/1200, of the Japanese battleships, Mutsu (1939), Haruna and Fuso (1942).

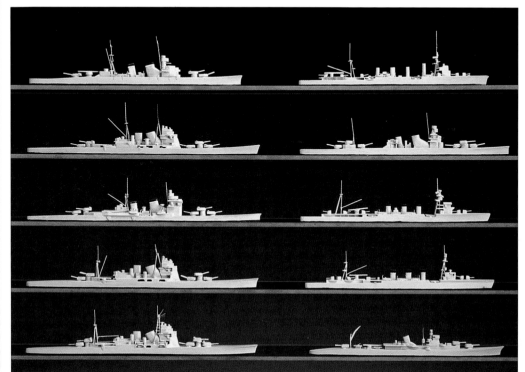

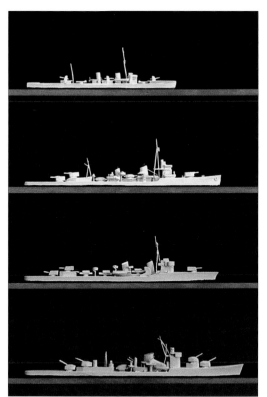

73. *Right. Russian battleship and cruisers to 1/1200 scale:* MAXIM GORKI, CHAPAEV, KRASNI KAUKAZ *and* MARAT.

75. *Far right. A close-up of the Russian cruiser* CHAPAEV, *painted in a strange greenish colour, and I believe one of the last recognition models to a 1/1200 scale to be made by Bassett-Lowke.*

71. *Japanese light cruisers to 1/1200 scale: the* KINUGASA, SENDI, MAYA, KAKO, NATI, NATORI, TAKAO, ATAGO *and* AGANO.

72. *Japanese destroyers to 1/1200 scale:* MOMI, KAGERO, SIRAKUMU *and* TERUTSUKI.

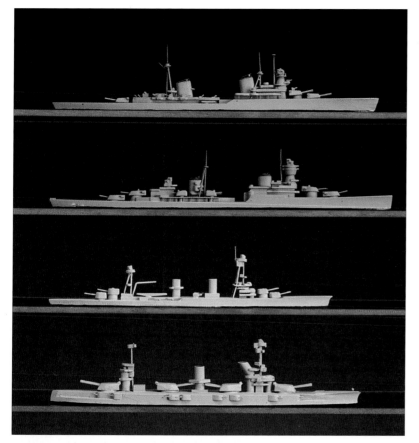

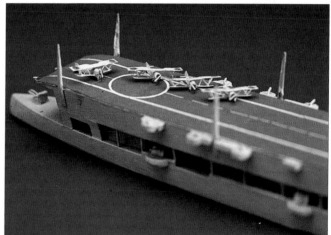

76. Above. The stern quarter of
HMS FURIOUS.

74. Left. The 1/1200 scale model of the
FURIOUS, which was issued in 1939 and is one
of the finest examples of work by Bassett-Lowke
in their recognition range. Swordfish aircraft are
shown on the flight deck.

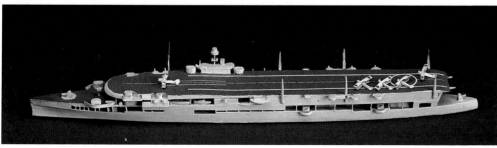

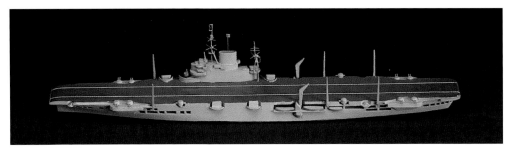

77. A 1/1200 recognition model of the VICTORIOUS which shows variations and modifications around the island, including a tripod mainmast.

78. An unusually detailed 1/1200 recognition model of the French seaplane carrier COMMANDANT TESTE. She was built in 1932 and, although scuttled at Toulon in November 1942, she was salvaged and refitted as a supply ship.

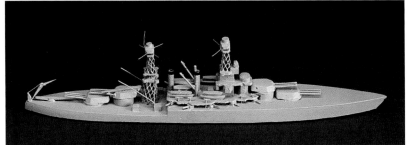

79. A 1/1200 recognition model of the TENNESSEE, numbered 52/137 and therefore issued to the RAF, very probably in 1940/41. The ship was at Pearl Harbour and was rebuilt giving her an entirely different profile with a single funnel.

80. HMS REPULSE to 1/1200 scale. This is an excellent recognition model, made in 1941, to the highest quality by Bassett-Lowke. The ship was sunk by Japanese dive bombers in the South China Sea on 10 December 1941.

81. A 1/600 (50ft. to 1in.) display case including models of the
ILLUSTRIOUS, KING GEORGE V, UGANDA and JAVELIN, as referred to
on page 32.

82. A contrast in size with two models of HMS ARETHUSA, one to 1/600 scale and the other at 1/1200.

83. Another pair of JAVELIN class destroyers, one at 1/600 scale with the other to 1/1200.

84. *The cruiser HMS* SHEFFIELD *in 1/1200 and 1/600 scales.*

85. *Left. A close-up of the 1/1200 scale HMS* SHEFFIELD, *which shows her after her 1952 refit to incorporate a lattice foremast.*

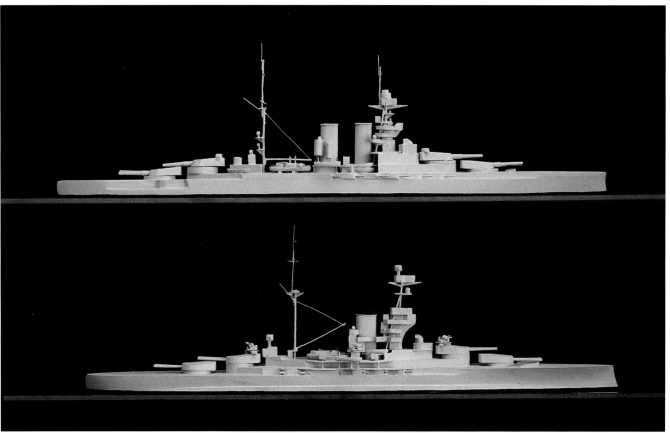

86. *The HMS* QUEEN ELIZABETH, *prior to refit in 1932, and HMS* ROYAL SOVEREIGN, *both models to a scale of 1/600.*

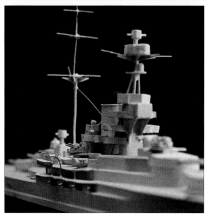

87. *Bow's view of HMS* ROYAL SOVEREIGN, *1/600 scale.*

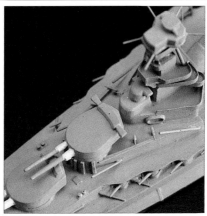

88. HMS WARSPITE (prior to 1937 refit)
and HMS NELSON,
both models to 1/600 scale.

89. 'A' and 'B' turrets of HMS WARSPITE,
1/600 scale.

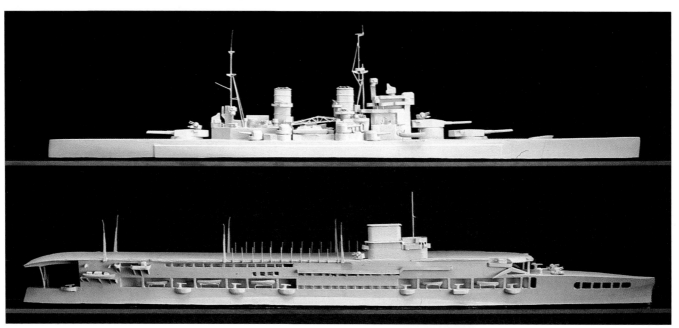

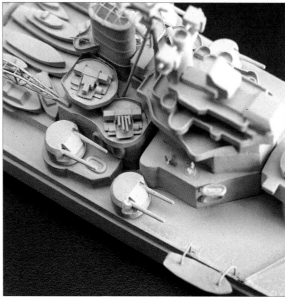

90. *HMS* KING GEORGE V *after refit in 1944 and HMS* GLORIOUS, *to 1/600 scale.*

91. *HMS* KING GEORGE V *to 1/600 scale.*

93. *Midship view, scale 1/600,*
of aircraft carrier HMS IMPLACABLE.

92. *Two WW2 British aircraft carriers to 1/600 scale –*
HMS IMPLACABLE *and* HMS GLORY.

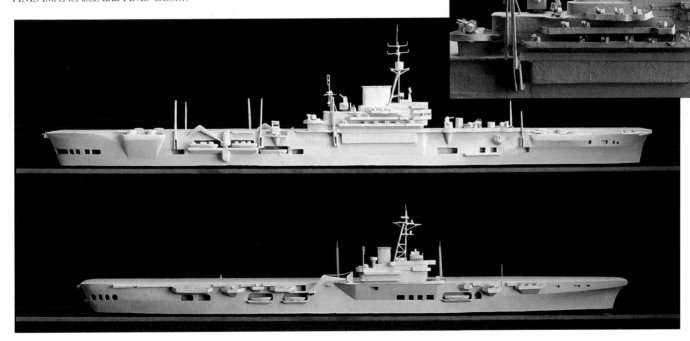

94. 1/600 scale recognition models of the British cruisers HMS Nigeria and HMS York.

95. Midships view of HMS York, 1/600 scale, with a 'Nimrod' float-plane on the catapult.

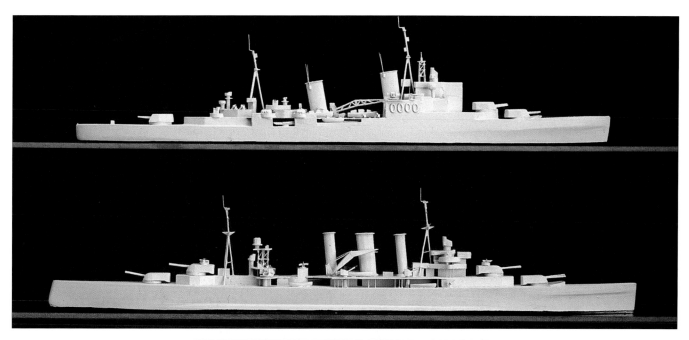

96. HMS SHEFFIELD and
HMS KENT to 1/600 scale.

97. Midship view
of HMS SHEFFIELD,
1/600 scale.

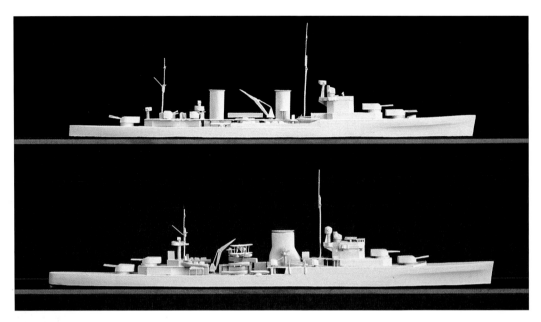

98. Scale recognition models of the ARETHUSA and LEANDER to 1/600 scale. The latter model shows a 'Walrus' amphibian on the mid-ships catapult.

100. Below. Recognition models of two pre-war cruisers to 1/600 scale – the HMS CAIRO and DUNEDIN.

99. Close-up of HMS LEANDER, scale 1/600, with 'Walrus' on midships catapult.

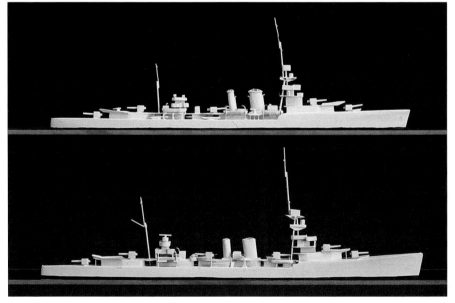

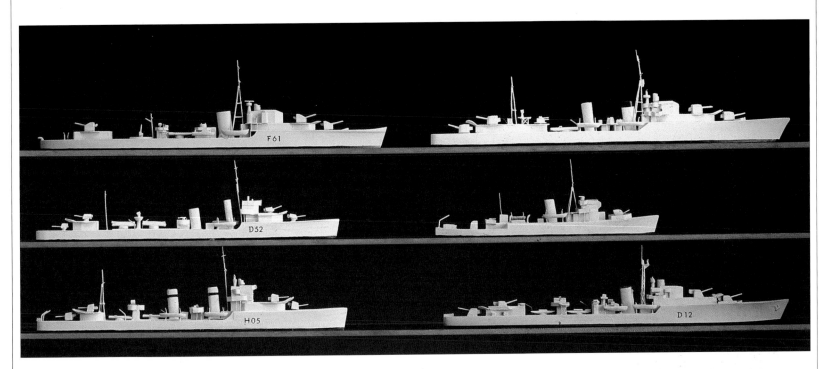

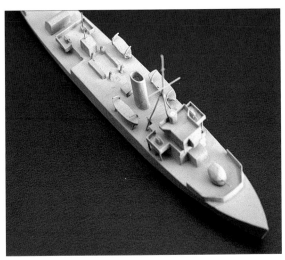

101. Wartime 1/600 recognition models of British destroyers and minesweeper: including JAVELIN, AFRIDI, VEGA, MARVEL, GREYHOUND and SAUMAREZ.

102. Left. The minesweeper HMS MARVEL, 1/600 scale.

103. Right. Midship section of 1/600 model of HMS JAVELIN. This was made by Miss Hughes during the last war for Bassett-Lowke (see page 26).

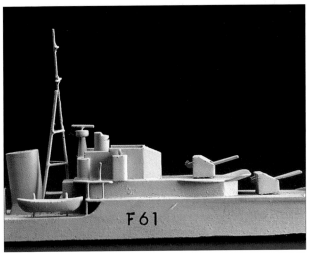

104. USN battleship NEW YORK to a scale of 1/600 made by Miss Judith Hughes.

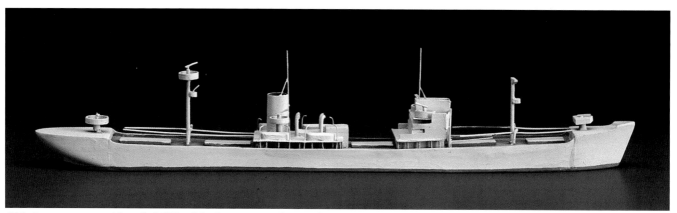

105. A recognition model, scale 1/600, of the German armed cargo ship SPERRBRECHER No.16. This ship was originally the Norwegian TULANE and was captured during the occupation of Norway and converted for anti-aircraft duties.

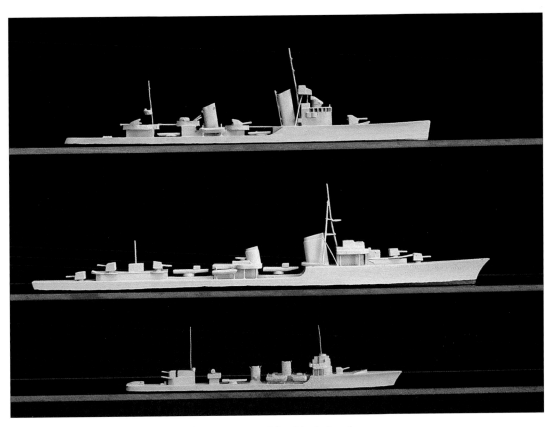

106. WW2 1/600 recognition models of the Italian destroyer
NAVIGATORE, the German destroyer NARVIK and the French destroyer
POMONE.

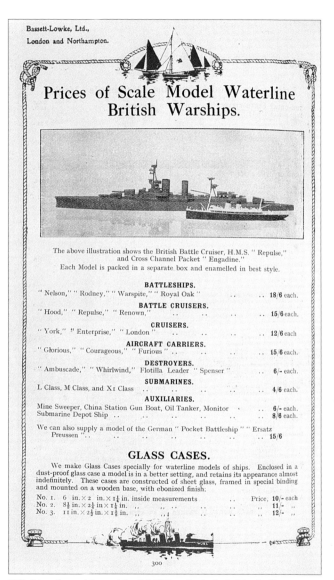

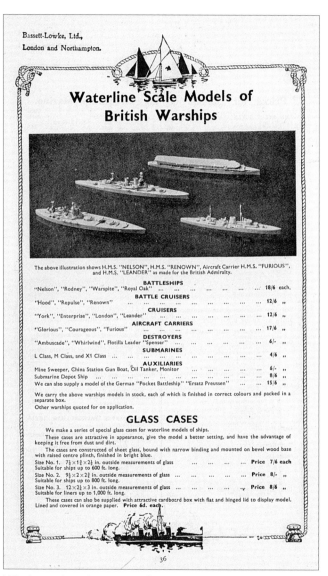

107. *List of warship models, 1/1200 scale, included in the Bassett-Lowke catalogue of 1933.*

108. *A page from the 1936 catalogue (see page 20).*

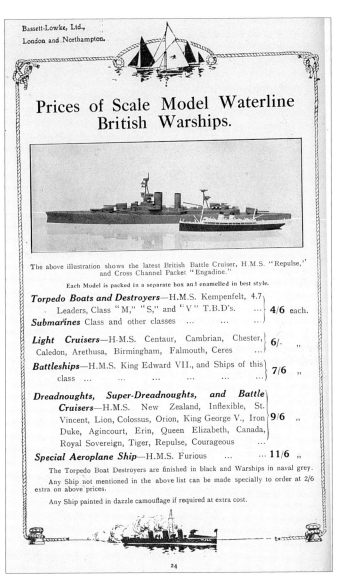

Bassett-Lowke, Ltd.,
London and Northampton.

Prices of Scale Model Waterline British Warships.

The above illustration shows the latest British Battle Cruiser, H.M.S. "Repulse," and Cross Channel Packet "Engadine."

Each Model is packed in a separate box and enamelled in best style.

Torpedo Boats and Destroyers—H.M.S. Kempenfelt, 4.7 Leaders, Class "M," "S," and "V" T.B.D's. **Submarines** Class and other classes ... ... } **4/6** each.

Light Cruisers—H.M.S. Centaur, Cambrian, Chester, Caledon, Arethusa, Birmingham, Falmouth, Ceres ...} **6/-** ,,

Battleships—H.M.S. King Edward VII., and Ships of this class ... ...} **7/6** ,,

Dreadnoughts, Super-Dreadnoughts, and Battle Cruisers—H.M.S. New Zealand, Inflexible, St. Vincent, Lion, Colossus, Orion, King George V., Iron Duke, Agincourt, Erin, Queen Elizabeth, Canada, Royal Sovereign, Tiger, Repulse, Courageous } **9/6** ,,

Special Aeroplane Ship—H.M.S. Furious ... **11/6** ,,

The Torpedo Boat Destroyers are finished in black and Warships in naval grey.

Any Ship not mentioned in the above list can be made specially to order at 2/6 extra on above prices.

Any Ship painted in dazzle camouflage if required at extra cost.

24

109. March 1923 catalogue, illustrating warships.

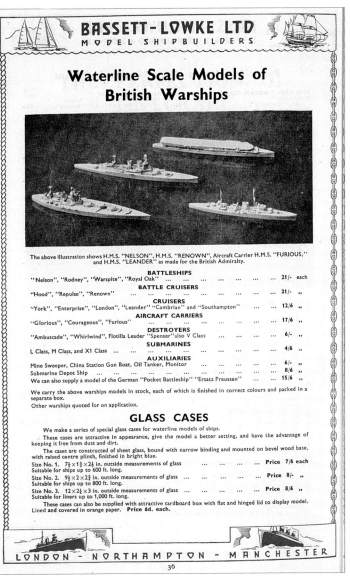

BASSETT-LOWKE LTD
MODEL SHIPBUILDERS

Waterline Scale Models of British Warships

The above illustration shows H.M.S. "NELSON", H.M.S. "RENOWN", Aircraft Carrier H.M.S. "FURIOUS," and H.M.S. "LEANDER" as made for the British Admiralty.

BATTLESHIPS	
"Nelson", "Rodney", "Warspite", "Royal Oak"	21/- each
BATTLE CRUISERS	
"Hood", "Repulse", "Renown"	21/- ,,
CRUISERS	
"York", "Enterprise", "London", "Leander" "Cambrian" and "Southampton" ...	12/6 ,,
AIRCRAFT CARRIERS	
"Glorious", "Courageous", "Furious"	17/6 ,,
DESTROYERS	
"Ambuscade", "Whirlwind", Flotilla Leader "Spenser" also V Class ...	6/- ,,
SUBMARINES	
L Class, M Class, and X1 Class	4/6 ,,
AUXILIARIES	
Mine Sweeper, China Station Gun Boat, Oil Tanker, Monitor ...	6/- ,,
Submarine Depot Ship	8/6 ,,
We can also supply a model of the German "Pocket Battleship" "Ersatz Preussen" ...	15/6 ,,

We carry the above warships models in stock, each of which is finished in correct colours and packed in a separate box.
Other warships quoted for on application.

GLASS CASES

We make a series of special glass cases for waterline models of ships.

These cases are attractive in appearance, give the model a better setting, and have the advantage of keeping it free from dust and dirt.

The cases are constructed of sheet glass, bound with narrow binding and mounted on bevel wood base, with raised centre plinth, finished in bright blue.

Size No. 1. 7½×1½×2½ in. outside measurements of glass ... ... **Price 7/6 each**
Suitable for ships up to 600 ft. long.
Size No. 2. 9½×2×2¾ in. outside measurements of glass ... ... **Price 8/- ,,**
Suitable for ships up to 800 ft. long.
Size No. 3. 12×2½×3 in. outside measurements of glass ... ... **Price 8/6 ,,**
Suitable for liners up to 1,000 ft. long.

These cases can also be supplied with attractive cardboard box with flat and hinged lid to display model. Lined and covered in orange paper. **Price 6d. each.**

LONDON - NORTHAMPTON - MANCHESTER

36

110. January 1940 catalogue of warships.

A CRAFTSMAN AT WORK   INSPECTING THE FINISHED MODEL

PRICE LIST

WATERLINE MODELS OF FAMOUS MODERN FIGHTING SHIPS
100 ft. to 1 inch

BRITISH

AIRCRAFT CARRIER

H.M.S. *Illustrious* 61/-

BATTLESHIPS

H.M.S. *King George V* .. 46/-
H.M.S. *Nelson* 46/-
H.M.S. *Renown* 46/-
H.M.S. *Queen Elizabeth* .. 50/-

CRUISERS

H.M.S. *Fiji* 33/6
H.M.S. *Dido* 33/6
H.M.S. *Southampton* .. 33/6
H.M.S. *London* 33/6
H.M.S. *Kent* 33/6
H.M.S. *Arethusa* 33/6

DESTROYERS

H.M.S. *Cossack* 19/6
H.M.S. *Castle* Class .. 19/6
H.M.S. *River* Class .. 19/6
H.M.S. *Hunt* Class .. 19/6

AMERICAN

AIRCRAFT CARRIER

Saratoga 61/-

BATTLESHIPS

North Carolina 46/-
Maryland 46/-
Alaska 46/-

CRUISERS

Baltimore 33/6
New Orleans 33/6
Augusta 33/6

111. *List of warship models, post-war catalogue.*

112. *Recognition models to 1/1200 scale of Dutch cruisers. The Tromp, completed in 1937: the Java of 1921; and the De Ruyter built in 1935 and sunk by the Japanese in 1942.*

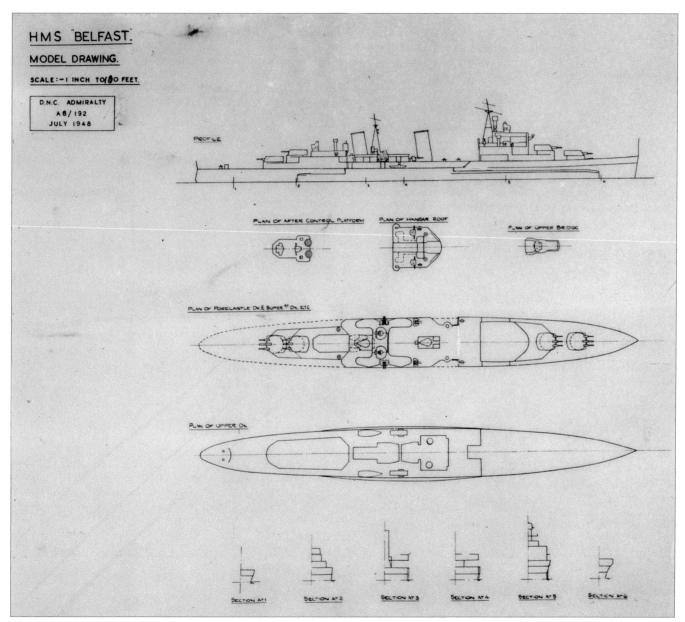

HMS "BELFAST."

MODEL DRAWING.

SCALE:- 1 INCH TO 80 FEET.

D.N.C. ADMIRALTY
A8/192
JULY 1948

PROFILE

PLAN OF AFTER CONTROL PLATFORM

PLAN OF HANGAR ROOF

PLAN OF UPPER BRIDGE

PLAN OF FORECASTLE DK & SUPER DK ETC

PLAN OF UPPER DK

SECTION AT 1

SECTION AT 2

SECTION AT 3

SECTION AT 4

SECTION AT 5

SECTION AT 6

113. Admiralty plan for HMS BELFAST for recognition models.

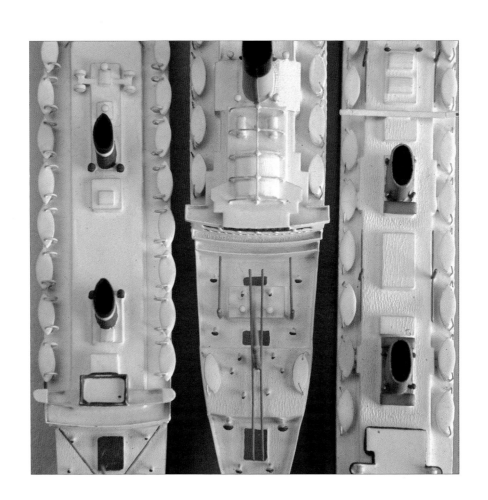

⇒THE MERCANTILE MARINE ⇐

Prior to 1920 Bassett-Lowke had tended to favour the production of warship models but after the end of WW1, the emphasis changed to merchant vessels. Warships had played their part in history and now was the time for trade, commerce and leisure, with special concentration on the major passenger liners that were bridging the 'old' and 'new' worlds across the Atlantic Ocean.

Today, when worldwide air travel is easily available to all, it is perhaps difficult to understand why ships were so important to passengers in the 1920s and 1930s. It should be remembered that voyages in liners often lasted for anything up to six weeks – a much longer time than most holidays these days – and the selection of the class of ship and its route became matters of considerable importance to the traveller. This was especially true of the North Atlantic trade, where there was keen competition between the rival shipping companies, whose giant liners contended for the prestigious 'Blue Riband'. National pride was also at stake.

Wenman Bassett-Lowke appreciated the situation and realised that there could be a lucrative market producing and selling miniature ship models to both passengers and shipping lines, with the additional prospect of tapping the collector's market as well.

In his *The Bassett-Lowke Story*, Roland Fuller refers to the success of marketing their warship models and being encouraged to expand into the field of the merchant fleet. It can be seen from the list of models in their 1923 catalogue that the initial range on offer was modest (see pp 96-97). Their optimism, however, was fully justified because only six years later, the list had expanded to cover some ninety vessels, from the three great ex-German giants, BERENGARIA, LEVIATHAN and MAJESTIC

114. Contrasts between the WASHINGTON, MAJESTIC and COLUMBUS all made to 1/1200 scale.

down to small cross-channel packets.

In the early twenties the models were fairly basic but sometimes detailed enough to include such things as boat davits, crow's nests and ship's cranes, etc. Towards the end of the decade, however, the skill and techniques of the craftsmen had greatly improved and by 1930 promenade deck windows were appearing on certain new models. These were achieved by means of a specially designed and purpose-built steel stamp which pressed out the requisite voids from thin Bristol board on to a lead base.

Such was the success of this enterprise that models of new ships were added to the range year by year until 1939. Extracts from Bassett-Lowke catalogues issued in 1932, 1936 and 1940 are included to illustrate the range of models available (pp. 98-101).

It is worth commenting on the development on some of the models made in this inter-war period. For example, both the BREMEN and EUROPA, Norddeutsche Lloyd's Atlantic record breakers, appeared during 1931, priced at the highest figure for that time of 37 shillings and 6 pence. The models showed both ships with their original squat funnels but their freeboard, the distance between upper deck and waterline, appeared to be unusually high. This was corrected in 1934 with the issue of revised models and the following year the same modified hulls were embellished with heightened funnels to match those of the full-sized ships, which had

115. A selection of early Bassett-Lowke merchant ship models made in the early 1920s. They are part of the comprehensive collection of Bassett-Lowke models owned by the American collector, Mr Poulos. Shown here are the IMPERATOR, AQUITANIA, OTRANTO, LUSITANIA and BRITANNIC. It can be seen that these models are very basic in finish compared with those produced by the firm in the 1930s.

been raised by some 25 feet to lift smuts clear of the after decks. Other models were also updated and improved, including Royal Mail Line's ATLANTIS, Orient Line's ORONSAY, Canadian Pacific's DUCHESS class, White Star Line's MAJESTIC and HOMERIC, and many others. In some cases bridge-wing houses or 'cabs' were added where none had been shown before, as with ATLANTIS and ORONSAY, while in others detail was refined or corrected. This was true of the famous French liner NORMANDIE, of which some 1,200 waterline models were built in all during her short life.

Variants of some ships also appeared, such as white-hulled cruising versions of Cunard's MAURETANIA and Canadian Pacific's EMPRESS OF SCOTLAND, whilst Blue Star Line's well-known cruise ship ARANDORO STAR appeared in several different guises. In 1937 models of Royal Mail Line's sister motor vessels ALCANTARA and ASTURIAS were re-issued with lengthened bow, raised funnels and new promenade deck windows, following their real counterparts' conversion to steam propulsion.

By the mid-1930s Bassett-Lowke were achieving the highest standards of model-making in the 100ft. to 1in. scale ever seen and all the models made at this time were superb in every respect. The quality of both detail and finish of representative models such as AWATEA (USSNZ), PRETORIA and WINDHUK (DOAL),

116. A group of post-war 1919 models from the collection of Mr Pierce Carlson, of London: the CAP TRAFALGAR *(1913-1914),* EMPRESS OF ASIA *(1913-1942) and the* KRONPRINZESSIN CECILE *(1906-1940). It is apparent that all these models are rather crude in finish and detail compared with those made in the next decade.*

MANHATTAN and WASHINGTON (US Lines), CHICHIBU MARU (NYK) and DOMINION MONARCH (Shaw Savill) has not, to my knowledge, been surpassed and they are a great tribute to the skill of the pre-war trio who made them: Jim Kent, Harold Denton and the Czech 'Harry' Checker.

Bassett-Lowke marketed their models from their own shops in Northampton, London and Manchester,

117. Other post-WW1 models produced in the early 1920s: the HILDEBRAND (compare this model with that made later No.97), the VIKING (ex ATRATO of the Royal Mail Line 1888-1914), the ST LOUIS (1895-1924) and the Dutch liner GELRIA (1913-1950).

with an additional franchise in Edinburgh in the early 1930s. Hamley's of Regent Street, the famous London toy shop, also sold these models for a few years in the mid-1930s, and it was there that I acquired my first Bassett-Lowke model, the ARANDORA STAR, before leaving for New Zealand in 1935.

Bassett-Lowke always offered to make models of any ship not listed in their catalogue, provided that plans and photographs were available. It is surprising how many were made, either singly or, as in the case of the Lamport Holt sisters VANDYK and VOLTAIRE, where I have seen three examples, in small batches of no more than half a dozen. These ranged from the Southern Railway's train ferry TWICKENHAM FERRY to the Norddeutsche Lloyd liner COLUMBUS, following her 1929 refit with squat motorship type funnels to bring her into line with her new running-mates BREMEN and EUROPA. A model of the COLUMBUS is shown in the catalogue before 1930 but this was of the earlier, rather basic type, showing the ship with her original tall funnels. Another rare model is that of the Italian liner AUGUSTUS of 1927, at that time the world's largest motor ship, which appears in only two catalogues prior to 1930.

One reason, perhaps, why individual ship models were ordered from Bassett-Lowke may have been that some passengers had enjoyed travelling in particular ships so much that they wanted to have a memento of their voyage. Small models were, after all, excellent souvenirs and were often sold in the ship's shop on board the vessel they represented. I obtained my models of P&O's MOOLTAN and STRATHAIRD in this way whilst returning from New Zealand in 1938, with a break for changing ships at Colombo. However, the first part of my journey across the Tasman Sea to Australia had been in the Union Steamship Company's beautiful AWATEA, of which I was unable to get a model as they were sold out. Happily, though, I was able to acquire one later.

Some fortunate children obtained these models as toys, though they did not take kindly to rough handling and their cost, which ranged from seven to 45 shillings (some £14 to £90 at today's values) usually put them out of reach of the younger generation.

To me, and I think to many others, these beautiful replicas are a reminder of the great days of the steamship era, when passenger liners and cargo vessels reflected in their varied and pleasing designs all that was

118. *Bassett-Lowke 1/1200 models of the Cunard Line:* AQUITANIA *(1914-1950),* MAURETANIA *(1907-1931),* MAURETANIA *(1932-1935) white hull,* BRENGARIA *(1922-1938),* SAMARIA *(1921-1956),* SAXONIA *(1900-1925),* FRANCONIA *(1922-1956),* AURANIA *(1924-1942),* AUSONIA *(1923-1939),* ANTONIA *(1922-1940).*

best in the naval architecture of that period.

Production of merchant ship models by Bassett-Lowke for commercial sale stopped early in 1940, when all resources were turned to the war effort, and the skills of their craftsmen were directed towards warship recognition models. It is largely due to their expertise that the subsequent naval models were finished to such high standards, way above all the models made by many other firms engaged in similar work during hostilities.

In addition to its ordinary clients, Bassett-Lowke also had some very well known patrons, enthusiastic collectors of model ships such as Lord Louis Mountbatten and Prince Chula Chakrabongse of Thailand, both of whom built up sizeable collections before the war. Many of those ordered by such collectors were specially made for them and Lord Mountbatten made a point of getting

119. 1/1200 models of the White Star Line: CERAMIC (1913-1942), DORIC (1922-1935), ALBERTIC (1927-1934), ADRIATIC (1907-1933), (from the collection of Lord Greenway), HOMERIC (1922-1936), OLYMPIC (1911-1935), a different model of ADRIATIC, CALGARIC (1922-1935), BRITANNIC (1930-1959) and GEORGIC (1932-1940).

120. 1/1200 models of the Canadian Pacific Railway & Steamship Co: the MONTROSE (1922-1939), EMPRESS OF AUSTRALIA (1922-1939), EMPRESS OF FRANCE (1919-1934), EMPRESS OF ASIA (1913-1941), DUCHESS OF ATHOL (1928-1940), DUCHESS OF YORK (1929-1943), EMPRESS OF BRITAIN (1931-1940) and the EMPRESS OF JAPAN (1930-1958).

121. Liners to 1/1200 scale of the P&O and Orient Lines. The ORFORD (1927-1940), ORONSAY (1925-1940), RANCHI (1925-1939), ORBITA (1919-1950) of the Pacific Steam Navigation Co., VICEROY OF INDIA (1929-1939), MOOLTAN (1923-1939), STRATHNAVER (1931-1939, service extended with one funnel to 1962), OTRANTO (1926-1940), ORCADES (1937-1940) and ORION (1935-1963).

models of all the ships he had served in. It is sometimes difficult to ascertain whether these 'specials' were made, before or after the war. Judging by the quality of workmanship it is generally safe to assume it would have been somewhere between 1932 and 1952, war years apart. It was during this period that the standard of workmanship achieved was at its peak as evidenced by the inclusion of promenade deck windows, superior

122. 1/1200 models of the Union Castle and Blue Star Lines: STERLING CASTLE *(1936-1965),* WARWICK CASTLE *(1930-1938),* ARANDORA STAR *(1929-1934),* ARANDORA STAR *(1936-1939),* ARANDORA STAR *(1934-1936),* ALMEDA STAR *(1926-1935),* ARUNDEL CASTLE *(1922-1937),* EDINBURGH CASTLE *(1910-1940),* ATHLONE CASTLE *(1936-1965) and the* CAPETOWN CASTLE *(1938-1967).*

detailing and a generally better finish.

Bassett-Lowke did, however, continue to produce some merchant ship models during the war, in parallel with the warship range, for instructional and recognition purposes. Miss Judith Hughes, for example, records having made the following, mainly axis-controlled, vessels for them during 1942: German 'HANSA' type liners,

'EIDER' class cargo ships (incidentally one of those finished in grey warpaint), as well as the freighter EHRENFELS and small passenger ship HELGOLAND; the Japanese freighter SAKITO MARU; the Italian cargo ship PIETRO ORSEOLO and fast, refrigerated units of the 'RAMB' class; and the French trans-Mediterranean passenger ship EL DJEZAIR and cross-Channel ferry COTE

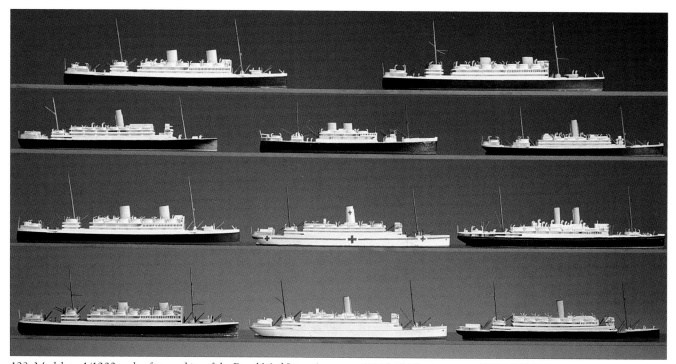

123. Models to 1/1200 scale of steamships of the Royal Mail Line: ASTURIAS (1935-1940), ASTURIAS (1926-1934), ALMANZORA (1920-1947), HIGHLAND CHIEFTAIN (1929-1959), ARAGUAYA (1906-1930), ALCANTARA (1935-1940), ATLANTIS as Hospital Ship, OHIO (1923-1927), ALCANTARA (1926-1934), ATLANTIS (1920-1939) and ARLANZA (1912-1938).

124. 1/1200 scale models of various lines: VOLTAIRE (1932-1939) of the Lambert & Holt Line, BELGENLAND (1923-1935) and PENNLAND (1925-1935) both of the Red Star Line, GLAUCUS (1921-1955) of the Blue Funnel Line, AWATEA (1936-1940) Union Steamship Co. of New Zealand, BRITANNIA (1926-1941) Anchor Line, HILDEBRAND (1911-1934) Booth Line, MONARCH OF BERMUDA (1931-1947) Furness Withy Line, DOMINION MONARCH (1939-1964) Shaw Savill & Albion Co. Ltd., and BERMUDA (1927-1931) also Furness Withy.

D'AZUR, which had been seized by the Germans. All of them were sent to Northampton for painting and Miss Hughes later work included a number of models of the new Cunard liner QUEEN ELIZABETH, finished in grey livery, to both 100ft. and 50ft. to 1in. scales, made in 1945-46.

Other wartime models that I have acquired or have seen, range from the twin-funnelled Norwegian liner OSLOFJORD, built in 1938 and sunk in December 1940, to the oil tankers ATHELDUCHESS, BEN READ and DL HARPER and the cargo vessels DUNKELD, EMPIRE HOPE, LOUISIANA, MATHIAS-STINNES and REICHENFELS.

In 1944, Bassett-Lowke supplied a large selection of 100ft. to 1in. liner and warship models to a Mr Hallas-Batchelor, who was producing a naval training film at Technicolour Ltd, Hounslow. I feel sure that somewhere these excellent models are still in existence and, hopefully, will one day come to light.

Other collections include the one at the Northampton Museum, presented by 'WJ' himself, and a similar one owned by Mrs Joan Derry, who was married to the Chairman of Bassett-Lowke. Both of these consist of specially-made wooden carrying cases which open out to reveal two rows of shelves on which are displayed 1/1200 scale models. These represent the development of the ship from early days, through sail and the coming of steam, up to and including the QUEEN ELIZABETH. One of the models, that of MAJESTIC, is a half model, enabling one to see her interior layout. Mr Bassett-Lowke used to use one of these portable show cases to illustrate lectures which he gave around the country on the history of the ship. In 1949 he published a booklet entitled *Progress of Transport by Water*, which

carried photographs of these particular models (see pp. 94-95).

Among the present day enthusiasts who have been collecting these 1/1200 ship models are Lord Greenway, who kindly allowed some of his impressive collection to be photographed for this book; Sir Patrick Wall, whose extensive collection is now housed in the Beverley Museum of Army Transport; and The Marquis of Aberdeen, whose collection also includes many present-day cast metal ship models.

In 1936, in addition to its fully finished models,

125. *Various 1/1200 passenger and cargo ships:* JESSMORE *(1941-1948),* REICHENFELS *(1937),* EL-DJEZAIR *(1933-1944),* MORMACPORT *(1942),* ATHOLDUCHESS *(1929),* EL KANTARA *(1932-1944),* SIR JAMES CLARK ROSS *(1930),* FREE ENTERPRISE I *(1962-1982) and* FREE ENTERPRISE II *(1963-1982).*

126. Liners of the United States Line
to 1/1200 scale, of the WASHINGTON
(1933-1951) and the LEVIATHAN
(1923-1938). The LEVIATHAN
was originally the German ship
VATERLAND, seized by the USA
in April 1917, after being interned in
New York from 1914. She then
became a US Navy transport
until her reconversion.

Bassett-Lowke also started to market some of them in
kit form. The superliners NORMANDIE and QUEEN
MARY were the chosen subjects and each kit was
packed in its own presentation box, with all components ready to assemble, including strips of promenade
deck windows and pre-painted funnels, which, in the
case of the NORMANDIE, were specially cast in brass.
The end result was designed to be similar to a standard
model of each liner in terms of quality but at the somewhat more affordable price of 12 shillings and six
pence. An even cheaper kit version, for the QUEEN
MARY only, was also available, priced at 7/6d. These
kits were only on sale for about four years and I have
only come across one example since 1940.

127. Bow's view of
1/1200 WASHINGTON.

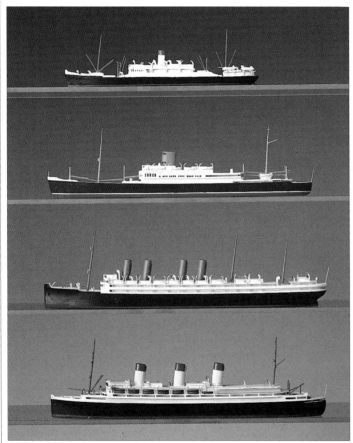

128. German liners to 1/1200 scale of the
Norddeutsche Lloyd and Hamburg Sud-
Amerika Lines: the GENERAL ARTIGAS
(1930-1943), SCHARNHORST (1935-1940),
KAISER WILHELM II (1903-1917) and CAP
ARCONA (1927-1940).

129. Additional Norddeutsche Lloyd models: COLUMBUS (1929-1939),
EUROPA (1930-1933), EUROPA (1933-1940)
and BREMEN (1933-1940).

130. Liners of the French Line (CGT) and other shipping companies
to 1/1200 scale: LAFAYETTE (1930-1938), COLOMBIE (1931-1940);
MOSELLA (1922-1953) and MASSILIA (1920-1944), both Cie Sud
Atlantique; ARAMIS (1932-1944), ANDRE LEBON (1913-1944) both
Messageries Maritime; FRANCE (1912-1934),
ILE DE FRANCE (1927-1947), NORMANDIE (1935-1943) and
CHAMPLAIN (1932-1940), all four of the French Line.

131. German liners to 1/1200 scale of the Hamburg-Amerika and German Africa Lines: the PRETORIA (1936-1945), CARIBIA (1933-1946), ST LOUIS (1929-1944), USAMBARA (1922-1945), RESOLUTE (1926-1935), WINDHUK (1937-1940), USARAMO (1920-1940), RELIANCE (1926-1938) and NEW YORK (1927-1934).

132. The beautiful Italian liner VICTORIA of the LloydTriestino Line, built in 1931. This model is one of the rarer ones produced by Bassett-Lowke as it was only marketed from 1938 to early 1940. The German liner MILWAUKEE of the Hamburg-America Line was built in 1929, and is shown in her white livery which she acquired in 1934 after refit as a luxury cruise liner. The company made models with both black and white hulls. One of the best models produced by this firm of the French liner L'ATLANTIQUE of the Cie Sudatlantique Line was completed in 1931. Not many replicas of this ill-fated ship were made, possibly because of her tragic end when she was destroyed by fire in 1933, after only two years in service. This is the only example that I have seen.

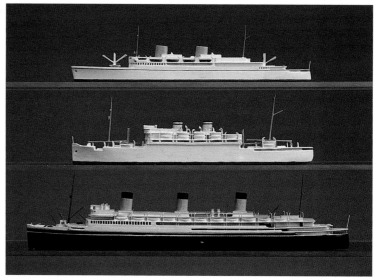

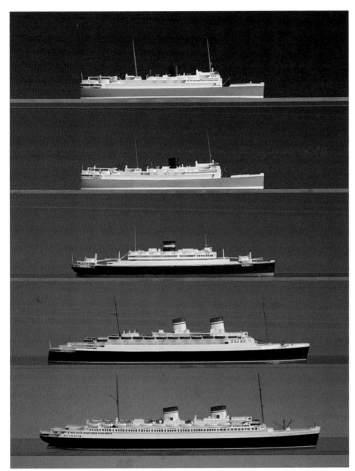

133. *Dutch and Italian Liners, 1/1200 scale, of the Rotterdam Lloyd and Italian Line: the* DEMPO *(1930-1940),* BALOERAN *(1930-1941),* VULCANIA *(1928-1937) in Cosulich Soc. Tristino di Nav. colours;* CONTE DI SAVOIA *(1932-1943) and* REX *(1932-1943).*

134. *Dutch and Japanese liners to 1/1200 scale: the* COLOMBIA *(1930-1942) Royal Netherlands Line,* STATENDAM *(1922-1939) and* NIEUW AMSTERDAM *(1938-1974) both Holland-America Line and* CHICHIBU MARU *(1930-1943) NYK Line.*

135. *A group of early 1930 models of the* MILWAUKEE *(1929-1946), the* NALDERA *(1920-1938) and the* MAURETANIA *in hospital ship livery.*

136. *An unusual collection of models specially made by Bassett-Lowke for a Belgian collector pre-1939, whose work included producing posters for the leading shipping companies of the world. These models survived the Second World War in Brussels and only surfaced in 1994. Part of this unique group of models includes the* ILE DE BEAUTE, *a French passenger-cargo ship of the Compagnie Fraissinet, which ran between Marseilles and Corsica (1930-1944); the Polish liner* PILSUDSKI, *sister to the* BATORY *(1935-1939); the Norddeutsche Lloyd liners* GENERAL VON STEUBEN *(ex* MUNCHEN *(1923-1945) and the* GNEISENAU *fitted with the 'bonnet' to her funnel (1936-1943).*

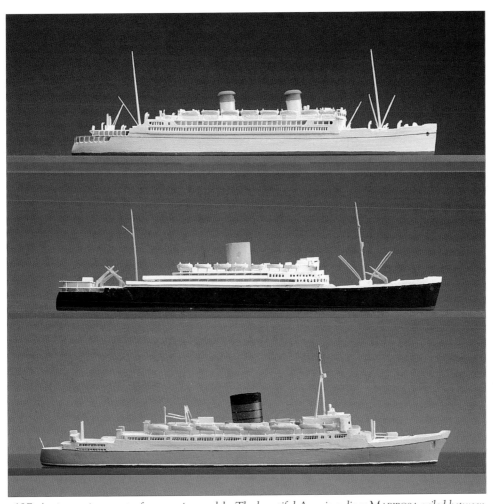

137. *An interesting group of contrasting models. The beautiful American liner* MARIPOSA *sailed between the western seaboard of the USA and Honolulu on to Sydney, Australia (1931-1974), the Royal Mail Line's* ANDES, *a post-war ship sailed between Southampton and La Plata following war service (1939-1971) and the Cunard liner* CARONIA *served mainly as a cruise liner (1948-1974).*

138. *1/1200 scale cross-channel vessels:* NORMANDIA, ISLE OF THANET, ANTWERP, BIARRITZ, MAID OF ORLEANS, MAID OF KENT, LORINA, WORTHING, PRINCE BAUDOUIN, VILLE DE LIEGE, TWICKENHAM FERRY *and* ISLE OF GUERNSEY.

139. *Further 1/1200 scale models of cross-channel vessels showing* ENGADINE, MALINES, VIENNA, ST BRIAC, BRITTANY *and* ANGLIA. *The latter three models were 'specials' as there is no record of any of them having been listed in any catalogue. The* ENGADINE *is an early model finished in the South-Eastern & Chatham Railway Company's livery, with white funnels and black tops.*

140. *Bassett-Lowke 1/1200 models of coastal and small craft:*
CUTTY SARK, *two tugs,* GLEN GOWER, YEWPARK *and* FULHAM.

141. *Waterline final assembly for* NORMANDIE
and QUEEN MARY *1935.*

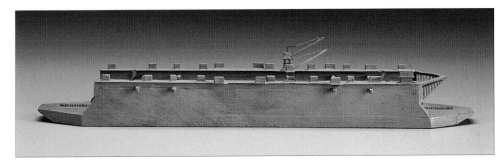

142. *The Floating Dock, marketed
by Bassett-Lowke between 1928
and 1931, to 1/1200 scale,
represented the one at Southampton
Docks.*

143. *The* MAJESTIC, *to 1/1200 scale,
appears to be unusual in the very high
quality of finish and detail, compared
with the standard models of this ship.
It is likely that this model was a
'special' made for some particular
order, which happened from time to
time.*

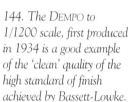

145. The AWATEA, 1/1200 scale, was introduced in 1936 and in my opinion is one of the finest models made by Bassett-Lowke of a very beautiful ship.

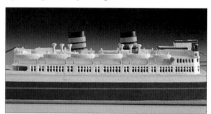

144. The DEMPO to 1/1200 scale, first produced in 1934 is a good example of the 'clean' quality of the high standard of finish achieved by Bassett-Lowke.

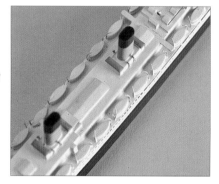

146. The HOMERIC to 1/1200 scale. Again this is a 'special' as the quality and detail surpasses that offered with the standard model. It is known that this particular model was made for Prince Chula Chakrabongse.

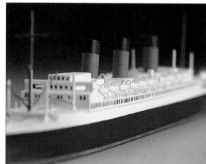

147. A delightful model to 1/1200 scale, of the ILE DE FRANCE of the French Line. The models of this ship were improved in quality from its introduction in the mid-1920s up to the start of WW2.

148. Close-up of the COLUMBUS, another model made especially for Prince Chula. This particular model was never listed with the ship having squat funnels.

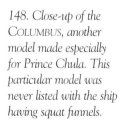

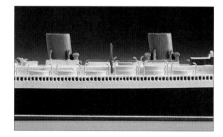

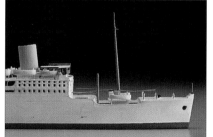

149. Part bows of STRATHNAVER.

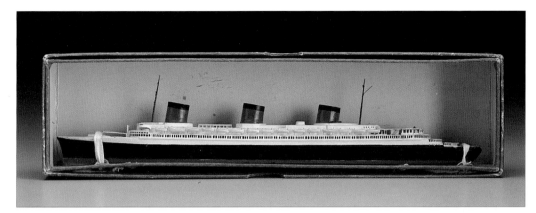

150. A boxed model of
NORMANDIE, scale 1/1200.
The models were secured
to the box with two tapes.

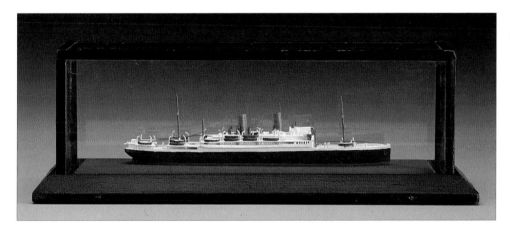

151. Glass case containing a 1/1200
model of SIERRA CORDOBA.

152. Glass case with a 1/1200 model
of the Australian ship CANBERRA.

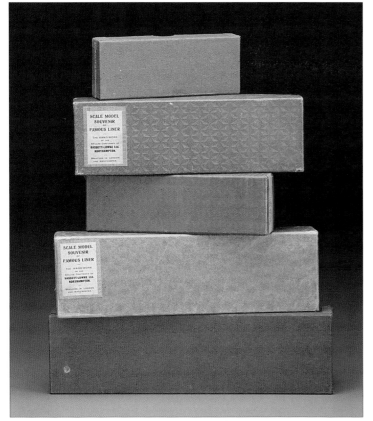

153. *The label, added to some boxes containing the larger merchant ships and liners, was placed at one end on the face of the box.*

154. *The distinctive orange box of the pre- and post-war periods. There were five sizes of this box to accommodate the smallest cross-channel boat to the largest liners. The war-time boxes, reduced to four different sizes, were of utility cardboard.*

155. *The end label, identical to that fixed to the base of the model, used for pre- and post-war boxes.*

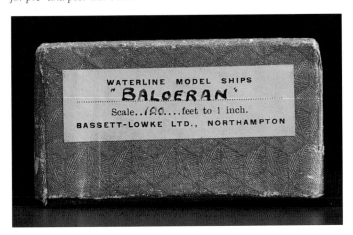

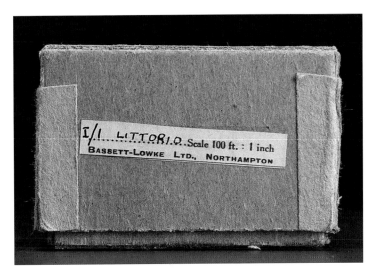

156. *Right. The label fixed to the base of a model.*

157. *Above. The war-time label for use with utility boxes.*

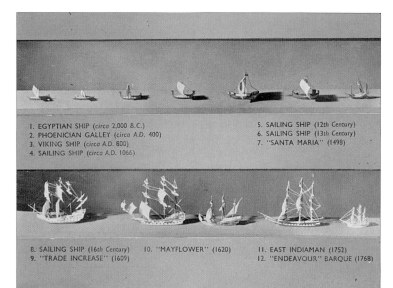

1. EGYPTIAN SHIP (circa 2,000 B.C.)
2. PHOENICIAN GALLEY (circa A.D. 400)
3. VIKING SHIP (circa A.D. 800)
4. SAILING SHIP (circa A.D. 1066)
5. SAILING SHIP (12th Century)
6. SAILING SHIP (13th Century)
7. "SANTA MARIA" (1498)

8. SAILING SHIP (16th Century)
9. "TRADE INCREASE" (1609)
10. "MAYFLOWER" (1620)
11. EAST INDIAMAN (1752)
12. "ENDEAVOUR" BARQUE (1768)

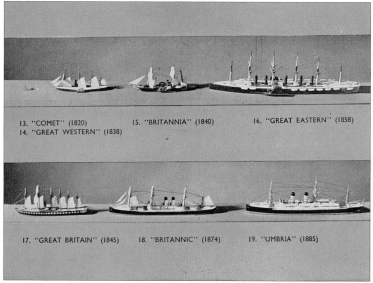

13. "COMET" (1820)
14. "GREAT WESTERN" (1838)
15. "BRITANNIA" (1840)
16. "GREAT EASTERN" (1858)

17. "GREAT BRITAIN" (1845)
18. "BRITANNIC" (1874)
19. "UMBRIA" (1885)

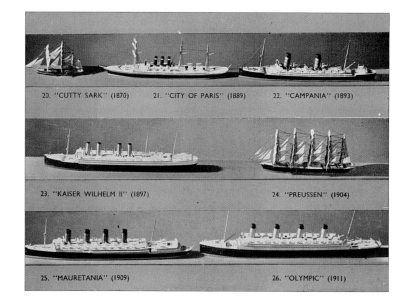

20. "CUTTY SARK" (1870)
21. "CITY OF PARIS" (1889)
22. "CAMPANIA" (1893)

23. "KAISER WILHELM II" (1897)
24. "PREUSSEN" (1904)

25. "MAURETANIA" (1909)
26. "OLYMPIC" (1911)

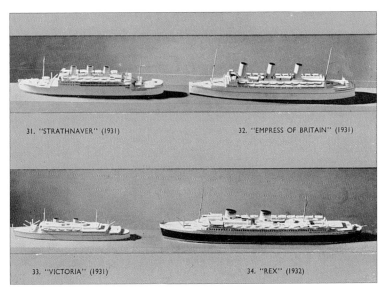

31. "STRATHNAVER" (1931)   32. "EMPRESS OF BRITAIN" (1931)

33. "VICTORIA" (1931)   34. "REX" (1932)

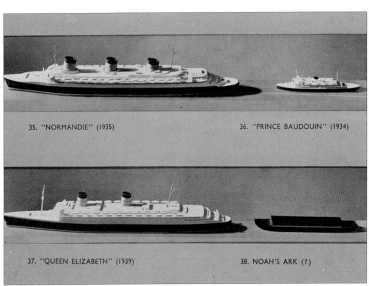

35. "NORMANDIE" (1935)   36. "PRINCE BAUDOUIN" (1934)

37. "QUEEN ELIZABETH" (1939)   38. NOAH'S ARK (?)

158-162. Left and above. Part of a collection of 1/1200 models used by Mr Bassett-Lowke when he was giving his lecture on 'Progress of Transport by Water'.

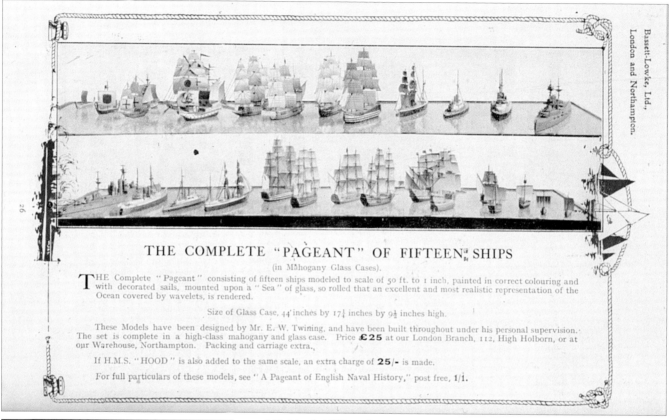

Bassett-Lowke, Ltd.,
London and Northampton.

THE COMPLETE "PAGEANT" OF FIFTEEN SHIPS

(in Mahogany Glass Cases).

THE Complete "Pageant" consisting of fifteen ships modeled to scale of 50 ft. to 1 inch, painted in correct colouring and with decorated sails, mounted upon a "Sea" of glass, so rolled that an excellent and most realistic representation of the Ocean covered by wavelets, is rendered.

Size of Glass Case, 44 inches by 17¼ inches by 9½ inches high.

These Models have been designed by Mr. E. W. Twining, and have been built throughout under his personal supervision. The set is complete in a high-class mahogany and glass case. Price **£25** at our London Branch, 112, High Holborn, or at our Warehouse, Northampton. Packing and carriage extra.

If H.M.S. "HOOD" is also added to the same scale, an extra charge of **25/-** is made.

For full particulars of these models, see "A Pageant of English Naval History," post free, 1/1.

163. March 1923 catalogue.

164. Contrasting 1/1200 scale models of the same ships. The Empress of Scotland, previously the German liner Kaiserin Augusta Victoria of the Hamburg-America Line, built in 1906. She was acquired in 1919 by Britain and after a few years with the Cunard Line joined the Canadian Pacific Railway Co. She is shown here in her trans-Atlantic and cruising livery of white hull, prior to the end of her service in 1930. The other two models show the Arandora, later the Arandora Star, of the Blue Star Line, at the start of her service to South America in 1927 and this ship altered for cruising at the end of her time just prior to WW2.

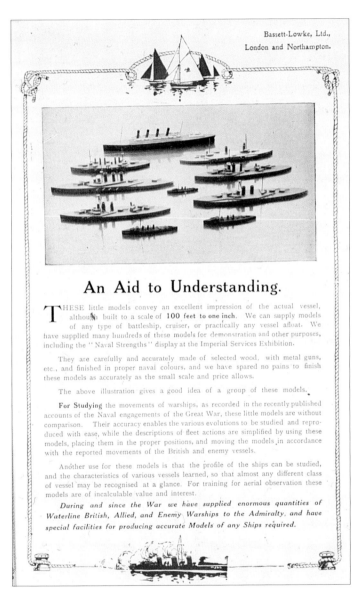

Bassett-Lowke, Ltd.,
London and Northampton.

An Aid to Understanding.

THESE little models convey an excellent impression of the actual vessel, although built to a scale of **100 feet to one inch**. We can supply models of any type of battleship, cruiser, or practically any vessel afloat. We have supplied many hundreds of these models for demonstration and other purposes, including the "Naval Strengths" display at the Imperial Services Exhibition.

They are carefully and accurately made of selected wood, with metal guns, etc., and finished in proper naval colours, and we have spared no pains to finish these models as accurately as the small scale and price allows.

The above illustration gives a good idea of a group of these models.

For Studying the movements of warships, as recorded in the recently published accounts of the Naval engagements of the Great War, these little models are without comparison. Their accuracy enables the various evolutions to be studied and reproduced with ease, while the descriptions of fleet actions are simplified by using these models, placing them in the proper positions, and moving the models in accordance with the reported movements of the British and enemy vessels.

Another use for these models is that the profile of the ships can be studied, and the characteristics of various vessels learned, so that almost any different class of vessel may be recognised at a glance. For training for aerial observation these models are of incalculable value and interest.

During and since the War we have supplied enormous quantities of Waterline British, Allied, and Enemy Warships to the Admiralty, and have special facilities for producing accurate Models of any Ships required.

165. March 1923 catalogue.

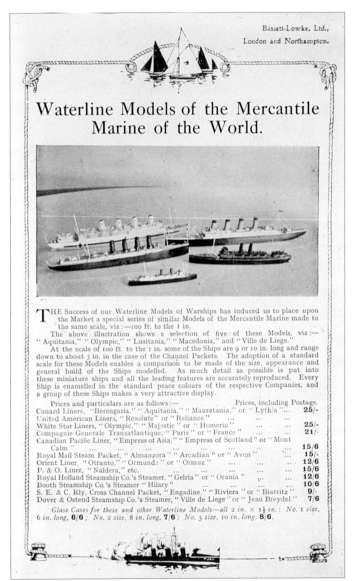

Bassett-Lowke, Ltd.,
London and Northampton.

Waterline Models of the Mercantile Marine of the World.

THE Success of our Waterline Models of Warships has induced us to place upon the Market a special series of similar Models of the Mercantile Marine made to the same scale, viz:—100 ft; to the 1 in.

The above illustration shows a selection of five of these Models, viz:—"Aquitania," "Olympic," "Lusitania," "Macedonia," and "Ville de Liege."

At the scale of 100 ft. to the 1 in. some of the Ships are 9 or 10 in. long and range down to about 3 in. in the case of the Channel Packets. The adoption of a standard scale for these Models enables a comparison to be made of the size, appearance and general build of the Ships modelled. As much detail as possible is put into these miniature ships and all the leading features are accurately reproduced. Every Ship is enamelled in the standard peace colours of the respective Companies, and a group of these Ships makes a very attractive display.

Prices and particulars are as follows:—   Prices, including Postage.

Cunard Liners, "Berengaria," "Aquitania," "Mauretania," or "Lythia" ...	**25/-**
United American Liners, "Resolute" or "Reliance"	
White Star Liners, "Olympic," "Majestic" or "Homeric"	**25/-**
Compagnie Generale Transatlantique, "Paris " or " France "	**21/-**
Canadian Pacific Liner, "Empress of Asia," " Empress of Scotland " or " Mont Calm "	**15/6**
Royal Mail Steam Packet, " Almanzora " " Arcadian " or " Avon " ...	**15/-**
Orient Liner, " Otranto," " Ormunde " or " Ormuz "	**12/6**
P. & O. Liner, " Naldera," etc.	**15/6**
Royal Holland Steamship Co.'s Steamer, " Gelria " or " Orania " ...	**12/6**
Booth Steamship Co.'s Steamer " Hilary "	**10/6**
S. E. & C. Rly. Cross Channel Packet, " Engadine," " Riviera " or " Biarritz "	**9/-**
Dover & Ostend Steamship Co.'s Steamer, " Ville de Liege " or " Jean Breydel "	**7/6**

*Glass Cases for these and other Waterline Models—all 2 in. × 1½ in.: No. 1 size, 6 in. long, **6/6**; No. 2 size, 8 in. long, **7/6**; No. 3 size, 10 in. long, **8/6**.*

166. March 1923 catalogue, illustrating liners.

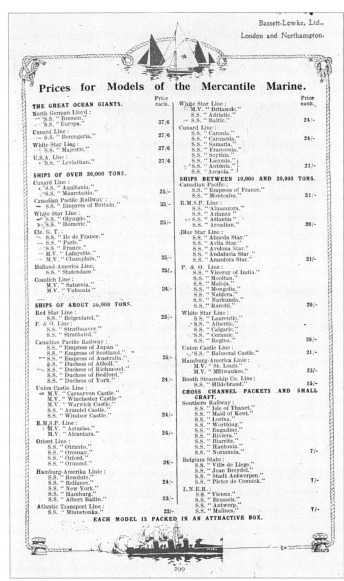

167. *May 1932 catalogue listing merchant ships.*

168. *Bassett-Lowke cover to Ships catalogue for October 1936.*

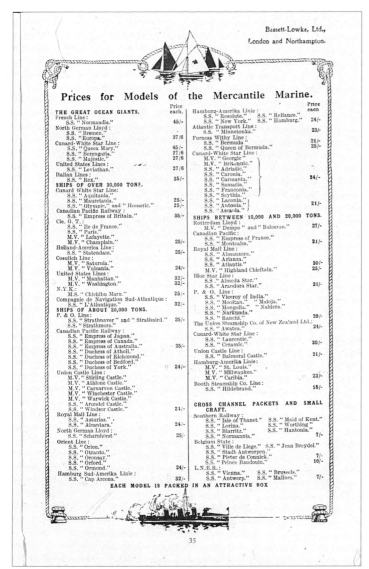

169. October 1936 catalogue listing liners and cross-channel craft.

170. January 1940 catalogue of merchant ships.

171. January 1940 catalogue of kits for QUEEN MARY and NORMANDIE.

172. January 1940 catalogue of 1/600 kits of CUTTY SARK and BRITANNIA.

BASSETT-LOWKE LTD
MODEL SHIPBUILDERS

ACCURATE SETS OF PARTS FOR MAKING SCALE WATERLINE MODELS

The increasing interest in the building of waterline models of famous ships has led us to introduce constructional sets of the two ships most in the eyes of the world at the moment.

"QUEEN MARY" SET

This is an inexpensive set of parts for constructing a 100 ft. to the inch model of the "QUEEN MARY". It has been produced by us in conjunction with Messrs. Handicrafts, Ltd., and is arranged for building by those who have had no previous experience in waterline model construction, yet at the same time in the hands of an experienced modeller produces an attractive and accurate souvenir of Britain's Queen of the Seas.

The set consists of hull roughly cut to shape, all deck fittings, lifeboats, ventilators, etc. Printed paper sheets shaped for building funnels, promenade deck windows, etc. Tube of adhesive, finished base for mounting, and glass, making complete show-case for the finished model. Complete in box with instructions.

Price 7/6   Postage 6d.

"QUEEN MARY" SET

Super quality, similar to "Normandie" set described below.
Price 12/6   Postage 6d.

"NORMANDIE" SET

This set makes up a standard "Bassett-Lowke" quality model of the famous holder of the Blue Riband of the Atlantic, scale 100 ft. to the inch. Every detail in the set is provided for, and many of the parts are completely finished. The funnels are painted ready for attaching, the lifeboats are hung on the davits, the decks are all cut to shape. The accessories include matt black and white enamel, tube of adhesive, tweezers, brush, glass-paper and holder, etc., and the whole is packed in an attractive box with a coloured illustration of the "NORMANDIE" on the box, supplied by courtesy of the French Line.

An excellent present for anyone who is keen on building models of ships.

Price 12/6   Postage 6d.

A Showcase for the Waterline Models "Normandie" and "Queen Mary"

A set of parts, including all the glass cut to size, shaped wood for the base and strapping for securing the glass in position, is supplied post free for 5/-.

BASSETT-LOWKE LTD
MODEL SHIPBUILDERS

A SCALE MODEL OF THE RENOWNED "CUTTY SARK"

The popularity of our 100 ft. to the inch sets of parts for building waterline models like the "Queen Mary" and "Normandie" has encouraged us to bring out a set of sailing ship parts and for this we have chosen the swift and graceful Clipper Ship "Cutty Sark", which is still to be seen in Falmouth Harbour—a training ship now for boys in the Mercantile Marine.

This set of parts is to a scale of 50 ft. to 1 in., making a model 4 in. long, and all the parts are numbered with full instructions, plans and drawings. The hull is ready shaped, with blue base, and the deck fittings cut, etc. Special material is provided for the sails, and also coils of black and white rigging cord. Also included in the set are paint brush, black and white paint, tweezers, and sandpaper block.

Price. Complete with illustrated instructions 12/6
    Finished Model in Glass Case 45/-
    Glass Case only 12/6
    Parts for making Glass Case 5/-
    Postage ... ... 6d.

THE CUNARDER
BRITANNIA

An exceptionally interesting addition to a ship lover's collection of the pioneers of the Atlantic run as she was the first Cunard Liner to make the crossing, on her maiden voyage July 4th, 1840.

Scale—1 in. to 50 ft.

This unique and complete Set of Parts includes the Shaped Hull, Masts, Sails, correctly painted Funnel, Boats, Paddle Boxes, Coloured Paddle Wheels, Deck Fittings and everything necessary to reproduce the model exactly as illustrated. A special feature is the inclusion of gilt replicas of the carved decorations on stem, stern and paddle boxes. These greatly enhance the finished model. The set also includes Scale Plans, full and clear Printed Instructions, Rigging, Coloured Wooden Base, Tools, Adhesive and Paint.

Price. 11/6
    Complete Model, in Glass Case (as illustrated) 45/-
    Finished Showcase 12/6
    Set of Showcase Parts 5/-

173. January 1940 catalogue of 1/600 kits of GREAT BRITAIN and GREAT EASTERN.

174. January 1940 catalogue with glass cases.

BASSETT-LOWKE LTD
MODEL SHIPBUILDERS

THE FAMOUS
"GREAT BRITAIN"

The first screw steamer to cross the Atlantic. Built in 1843 by the famous Brunel for the Great Western Steamship Company. The most daring ship of her time, built of iron, with a tonnage of 3,448 in the old measurement.
This attractive model set is to a scale of 50 feet to 1 inch and includes Shaped Hull, Sails, Deck Parts and Masts, Scale Plans, Printed Instructions, Tools and Paint. Model 6 inches long.

Set of Parts as described ...	11/6
Finished Model in Glass Case ...	45/-
Finished Glass Case ...	12/6
Set of Parts for making Glass Case	5/-

THE
"GREAT EASTERN"

Brunel's historic experiment in Propulsion by Sail, Screw and Paddle. Built for Far East traffic, her delayed launch proved costly and she was sold to the Great Ship Company for North Atlantic traffic. Famous for laying the Atlantic Cable.

Scale 50 feet to one inch. Set of parts, including Carved Hull, Decking, Scale Parts, Funnels, Masts, Sails, Plans, Special Instructions for Building, Tools and Paint ... ... Complete	14/6
Finished Model in Glass Case ...	50/-
Finished Glass Case	12/6
Set of Parts for making Glass Case	8/-

SUNDRIES FOR WATERLINE MODELLERS

PROMENADE DECK WINDOWS. In strips of six different sizes, suitable for 100 ft. to 1 in. models. Price per Strip, 3d.
LIFEBOATS. With or without Davits, Six different Sizes. To suit Model Ocean Liners to the scale of 1 in. to 100 ft.
Price per dozen complete, 9d.
SHOWCASE PARTS. To build yourself. Glass cut to size, ready shaped wooden base, strappings, etc. Mahogany finish.
Price (Usual Size), 5/-
For "Great Eastern", 8/-
PAINTS for Models Ships. As used in our own works. Red, Yellow, Black and White. By judicious mixing practically all shades needed can be obtained. Two inch Tubes, 6d. each. Four inch Tubes, 9d. each.

LONDON - NORTHAMPTON - MANCHESTER

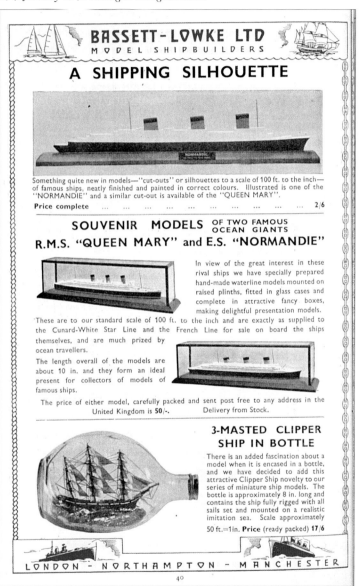

BASSETT-LOWKE LTD
MODEL SHIPBUILDERS

A SHIPPING SILHOUETTE

Something quite new in models—"cut-outs" or silhouettes to a scale of 100 ft. to the inch—of famous ships, neatly finished and painted in correct colours. Illustrated is one of the "NORMANDIE" and a similar cut-out is available of the "QUEEN MARY".

Price complete **2/6**

SOUVENIR MODELS OF TWO FAMOUS OCEAN GIANTS
R.M.S. "QUEEN MARY" and E.S. "NORMANDIE"

In view of the great interest in these rival ships we have specially prepared hand-made waterline models mounted on raised plinths, fitted in glass cases and complete in attractive fancy boxes, making delightful presentation models.

These are to our standard scale of 100 ft. to the inch and are exactly as supplied to the Cunard-White Star Line and the French Line for sale on board the ships themselves, and are much prized by ocean travellers.

The length overall of the models are about 10 in. and they form an ideal present for collectors of models of famous ships.

The price of either model, carefully packed and sent post free to any address in the United Kingdom is **50/-.** Delivery from Stock.

3-MASTED CLIPPER SHIP IN BOTTLE

There is an added fascination about a model when it is encased in a bottle, and we have decided to add this attractive Clipper Ship novelty to our series of miniature ship models. The bottle is approximately 8 in. long and contains the ship fully rigged with all sails set and mounted on a realistic imitation sea. Scale approximately 50 ft.=1in. **Price** (ready packed) **17/6**

LONDON - NORTHAMPTON - MANCHESTER

～ POST WW2 PERIOD ～

Probably like many others, I believed that once the war was over, Bassett-Lowke would quickly resume production of their miniature waterline ship models on the same basis as before but for some reason, which I have never been able to understand, this never happened. Perhaps it had something to do with the shortage of materials or just the general austerity of the period. At any rate a small catalogue appeared in 1946, listing some 14 models which had been available before the war, together with five additional ones of ships completed just prior to or soon after the outbreak of hostilities, namely Cunard's QUEEN ELIZABETH, Royal Mail's ANDES, US Line's AMERICA, Compagnie Sud Atlantique's striking PASTEUR, with her huge single funnel, and Nederland Line's triple screw motor ship ORANJE. Also listed were a further 19 models, which had been held over during the war and were now

released for sale. These soon sold out and disappeared from subsequent catalogues, the last of which was issued in 1950. I have included an extract from this small brochure and in one illustration can be seen a model of the Great Lakes passenger steamer MILWAUKEE CLIPPER alongside the AMERICA. The former was one of three specially made for Bassett-Lowke by Judith Hughes.

As far as I can establish, the last set of commercial models made as 'standards' were of US Line's record-breaking liner UNITED STATES, which in 1952 easily wrested the Blue Riband from the QUEEN MARY with an astonishing average speed of over 35 knots. Only six of these were produced and they followed runs of Cunard's two 'QUEENS', the new MAURETANIA and the CARONIA. By 1960 there were no other models from either the pre-or post-war catalogues available, as all had been sold out. Illustrated on page 17 is a copy of a letter

175. The 1/1200 model of the UNITED STATES with the model length 10 inches.

received from Bassett-Lowke in April 1955, listing and pricing the only models then for sale. It can be seen that the cost of a 1/1200th model of QUEEN ELIZABETH had risen from £4.15.0 in 1947 to 5 guineas in 1949 and had subsequently doubled to 10 guineas by 1955.

176. 1/1200 post-war Bassett-Lowke models of the GEORGIC (1949-1955), PASTEUR (1939-1956), AMERICA (1946-1964) and MAURETANIA (1939-1963). The PASTEUR is one of the many models kindly lent for these photographs from the extensive collection of Lord Greenway.

An enquiry some seven years later, in June 1962 to be precise, revealed that the cost of a 'special' had reached £25. To go further, a friend who used to visit Northampton from time to time in the late 1970s, was informed in answer to a similar query that the cost of the man hours alone would amount to about £60.

Among the specials I have been able to collect or have seen in other collections, are such models as Cunard's intermediate liner CARINTHIA (1956); Royal Mail's AMAZON (1959); Shaw Savill's emigrant ship NEW AUSTRALIA, converted from the QUEEN OF BERMUDA in 1949; Furness Withy's OCEAN MONARCH (1950); Anchor Line's BRITANNIA (1926); Canadian Pacific's three-funnelled PRINCESS MARGUERITE (1925) and Messageries Maritimes' square-funnelled motor ship ARAMIS (1932) to name but a few.

It has already been said that more than one craftsman was involved in making these miniature ship models, but, nevertheless, in the decade preceding WW2 a certain standardisation of quality and finish was achieved. However this was not to be the case later, as we shall see. As mentioned earlier, during the war, Bassett-Lowke employed sub-contractors to meet the greatly increased demand and some were commissioned for similar work after the war. This does not in any way imply that the work of these sub-contracting firms was

177. The Furness, Withy Line's OCEAN MONARCH *of 1951. I have seen two examples of this model. One is shown here, the other being in Lord Greenway's collection. It was purchased by him in the early 1950s at the Bassett-Lowke shop in High Holborn, London. I suspect that very few were made of this attractive liner which ended her service in 1966. The French liner* LIBERTE, *once the pre-war German liner the* EUROPA, *went into service with C.G.T. in 1950. This model could have been a special order, but is probably one of a batch made by B-L for the French Line, either late in the 1940s or early 1950s. This theory is supported by the fact that Miss Judith Hughes completed sixty models in 1950 for Bassett-Lowke for the French Line of the two funnel refitted* ILE DE FRANCE. *The model of the* LIBERTE *would be complimentary covering the new additions to the Line's post-war major liners.*

inferior to the B-L models but any model-maker places his own individual stamp on his workmanship. This is why, perhaps, one finds that models of a particular ship vary in detail and finish, but not necessarily in quality. This point can be illustrated by the photographs of three 1/1200th models of the QUEEN ELIZABETH on page 108. The first is a grey painted wartime example made for the Admiralty, the second post-war one is identical, save for being painted in Cunard colours, and is the same as that illustrated in the mini-catalogue, whilst the third was, I suspect, produced in the early 1950s. It can be seen that the first two differ from the third in upper deck detail and particularly in the number of lifeboats fitted. The last one is correct and no one at Bassett-Lowke could ever explain to me why the earlier models were short of two lifeboats, one on either side, even though larger

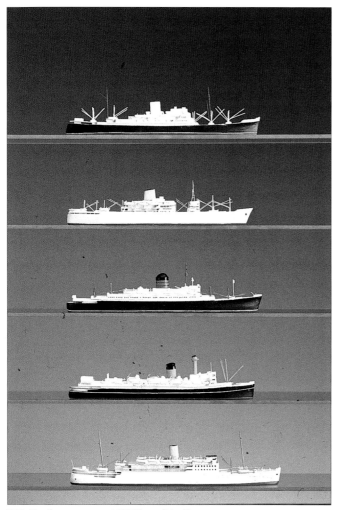

176. Further post-war 1/1200 models: RANGITOTO (1949-1969), AMAZON (1959-1968), CARINTHIA (1956-1968), NEW AUSTRALIA (1949-1958) and STRATHNAVER (1948-1962).

models of the same ship, produced to 50ft. and 25ft. to 1in. scales at the same time, were accurate.

Mr Kent continued to work on small-scale ship models in the immediate post-war period and he was joined in this work by Mr Richard (Dick) Shrives, who was responsible for all the paintwork. Ordinary commercial eggshell paint was used to which was added just a touch of gloss. A model would receive two coats of white undercoat and then, using a wide brush, a single coat of hull colour would be applied in a single sweep around both sides, with no masking! Both Denton and Checker had by this time retired due to old age and Jim Kent's work in this field was limited due to other demands on the company's resources. Consequently Bassett-Lowke was again placed in the position of having to seek assistance from outside to meet orders for waterline models between 1947 and approximately 1955.

One such sub-contractor was Mr Leslie Osbourne, a ship modelmaker who had moved from East London to Christchurch in Dorset. Before he died he told me that he had helped out Bassett-Lowke in the years just after the last war but I do not believe he produced models for them in any great quantity. Another expert craftsman was Mr Kim Allen of Westerham, Kent, who also assisted Bassett-Lowke in a small way. I had previously met Mr Allen in 1945 in New Delhi, when, as an RAF squadron leader, he was commanding the photographic and topographic unit making models, including ships, for South East Asia Command.

Miss Judith Hughes' longstanding association with the company has already been mentioned but in 1950 she produced for them in her Devon workshop 60 models of the rebuilt ILE DE FRANCE, following an order received from the French Line. Mr Ron Hughes, no relation incidentally and a very successful present day modelmaker, has informed me that another post-war

sub-contractor was a Mr Jim Lillywhite, who died in the late 1960s, but regrettably I never had the opportunity of either meeting or talking to him.

Sadly, these small models are today becoming scarce and difficult to obtain, with the result that they command high prices when they do turn up, either singly or in collections, at auction or in antique shops or markets. Sometimes they surface in very strange ways. For example, some years ago Mr Mike Fielding, the managing director of Bassett-Lowke, telephoned me to say that he

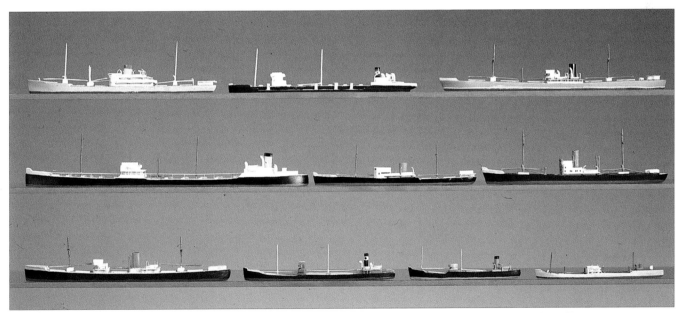

177. WW2 and post-war 1/1200 cargo ships and tankers: KLIPPAREN, CRIOLLO FIEL, QUEEN MAUD, RL HAGUE, ULM, EIDER, CAPE CLEAR, CORHAMPTON, MARQUIS and HOMBURG coaster.

178. WW2, 1/1200 scale recognition models of the QUEEN ELIZABETH. I have never seen any evidence
that this ship was dazzle painted and the model may have been used as a trial painting.

179. The post-war commercial models, scale 1/1200, of the QUEEN ELIZABETH. The top model was made
in 1947 and the lower one in the early 1950s, the latter being the correct version (see p.105).

had been approached by a couple who had bought a cabinet at auction and later discovered that one of its drawers contained about a dozen merchant ship models, together with some Bassett-Lowke harbour accessories, including tugs, cranes and warehouses. They had found the identifying labels under the models and, as they lived in Northampton, had approached the company to seek advice on what they had unwittingly acquired. I was most pleased to assist with the disposal of this valuable haul!

A more recent example of the curious way models can still surface many years after they were acquired,

happened in 1993. A widow of a Marine Insurance Agent, whose husband had died some twenty years before told her gardener in the late 1980s to clear out her garage and keep anything that he wanted. He found there some twenty-five ship models, mainly of the larger liners of the mid-war period, all made by Bassett-Lowke to their standard scale of 100ft. to 1in. These models then went into his loft where they remained until the gardener's son decided to turn out the attic, found the models carefully packed away and took them to a leading auctioneer who identified them and included them in the nearest appropriate sale.

180. In the foreground is the MILWAUKEE CLIPPER scale 1/1200, one of three, two of which were made by Miss Judith Hughes for Bassett-Lowke in October 1944. A contrast in size is the UNITED STATES, also at 1/1200 scale, which was the last commercial model made by Bassett-Lowke. Only six were produced in 1952/53.

One great advantage of collecting small 100ft. to 1in. scale waterline models is that, due to their small size – between 2 inches and 10 inches in length, they can be easily exhibited in the home, taking up little space, and are at the same time both attractive and interesting to look at. They conjure up nostalgia for the great days of shipping, especially to those who remember the pre-war era and who might also have travelled in some of the ships the models represent. Bassett-Lowke justifiably claimed that they were 'perfection in miniature' and they are a fitting memorial to the skilled workmanship of the craftsmen of those days.

By way of a postscript, the last models that I purchased direct from the company, as a special order, were the Townsend car ferries FREE ENTERPRISE I and FREE ENTERPRISE II in 1966.

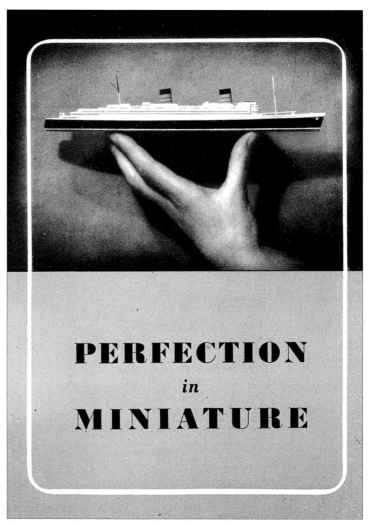

181. Cover to the post-war catalogue, first issued in 1947.

ATLANTIC BLUE RIBAND HOLDERS...

This group of 50 ft. to 1 in. miniatures of modern ocean giants is being reviewed by a model of the *Santa Maria*, the first vessel in which Columbus crossed the Atlantic and discovered a new continent.

A Group of Waterline Models, to the same scale as our standard productions illustrated on pages 2–7, viz. 100 ft. to 1 in. or 1/1200th actual size.

MEMORIES OF 'D-DAY'—A SELECTION OF LANDING CRAFT MODELS

R.M.S. QUEEN ELIZABETH   (CUNARD WHITE STAR)

The world's largest and fastest ship, completed by John Brown of Clydebank in 1940. Propulsion: geared turbines. Length 1,029 ft. Beam 120 ft. Gross tonnage 84,000. Speed ? Length of model 10¼ in.   Price £5 5 0

R.M.S. QUEEN MARY   (CUNARD WHITE STAR)

The *Normandie*'s challenger on the North Atlantic express service. Maiden voyage May 1936. Propulsion: geared turbines. Length 1,018 ft. Beam 118 ft. Gross tonnage 81,235. Speed 30 knots. Length of model 10 in. Price £5 5 0

E.S.S. NORMANDIE   (COMPAGNIE GÉNÉRALE TRANSATLANTIQUE)

The pride of France and one of the most beautiful ships in the world. Propulsion: turbo-electric. Length 1,029 ft. Beam 119 ft. Gross tonnage 83,243. Speed 30 knots. Length of model 10¼ in.

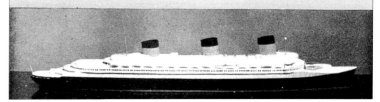

182&183. Pages from the 1947 catalogue.

R.M.S. EMPRESS OF BRITAIN (CANADIAN PACIFIC)

The largest and fastest ship in the Canadian service and a luxury cruising vessel. Built in 1931. Propulsion: geared turbines. Length 759 ft. Beam 97 ft. Gross tonnage 42,348. Speed 24 knots. Length of model 7½ in.

S.S. BREMEN (NORDDEUTSCHER LLOYD)

With her sister ship *Europa*, Germany's finest ships and the first successful attempts at streamline design. The *Bremen* was built in the Weserwerke, Bremen, in 1929. Propulsion: geared turbines. Length 938 ft. Beam 98 ft. Gross tonnage 51,656. Speed 28 knots. Length of model 9⅜ in.

NIEUW AMSTERDAM (HOLLAND-AMERIKA)

One of the finest and most beautiful ships afloat. Built at Rotterdam in 1938. Propulsion: geared turbines. Length 751 ft. Beam 88 ft. Gross tonnage 36,200. Speed 27 knots. Length of model 7½ in. Price £3 17 0

REX (ITALIA LINES)

Italy's finest ship, built by the Soc. Anon. Ansaldo, Genoa in 1932. With the *Conte de Savoia* built at Trieste, she put Italian shipping on a par with the best in the world. Propulsion: geared turbines. Length 880 ft. Beam 97 ft. Gross tonnage 51,062. Speed 28 knots. Length of model 8¾ in.

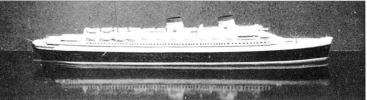

STRATHAIRD (PENINSULAR AND ORIENTAL)

With her sister ship the *Strathnaver*, well-known on the Far Eastern service. Built by Vickers Armstrong of Barrow-in-Furness in 1931. Propulsion: turbo-electric. Length 639 ft. Beam 80 ft. Gross tonnage 22,300. Speed 22 knots. Length of model 6⅜ in. Price £2 18 0

R.M.S. BRITANNIC (CUNARD WHITE STAR)

With the *Georgic*, Britain's largest motor-ships. Built by Harland & Wolff in 1930. Propulsion: Diesel motors. Length 712 ft. Beam 82 ft. Gross tonnage 26,947. Speed 18 knots. Length of model 7 in.

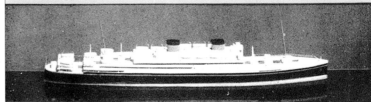

184&185. Post-war catalogue, illustration of models.

H.M.S. ATHLONE CASTLE (UNION CASTLE LINE)

One of the express service ships to South Africa. Striking vessels with lavender hulls, white upper work and red-and-black funnels. Built by Harland & Wolff of Belfast in 1936. Propulsion: Diesel motors. Length 680 ft. Beam 82 ft. Tonnage 25,500. Speed 19 knots. Length of model 6¾ in. Price £2 18 0

M.V. DOMINION MONARCH (SHAW-SAVILL AND ALBION)

The largest and finest vessel engaged on the England-New Zealand service via Cape Town and Durban. Completed by Swan Hunter & Wigham Richardson in 1939. Propulsion: geared turbines. Length 682 ft. Beam 85 ft. Gross tonnage 27,200. Speed 19½ knots. Length of model 6¾ in. Price £3 12 0

R.M.S. ANDES (ROYAL MAIL LINES)

A beautiful ship built in 1939 for the luxury service between England and South America. Propulsion: geared turbines. Length 669 ft. Beam 83 ft. Gross tonnage 25,000. Speed 25 knots. Length of model 6¾ in. Price £2 18 0

PASTEUR (SUD ATLANTIQUE)

A luxury ship built for the Bordeaux-South American Service, but now operated by the Cunard White Star Line. Completed in 1939 by the Soc. des Chantier et Ateliers de St. Nazaire Penhoet. Propulsion: geared turbines. Length 696 ft. Beam 88 ft. Speed 25 knots. Length of model 7 in.

AMERICA (UNITED STATES LINES)

The largest merchant ship built in the U.S.A. and completed just before America entered the war. Propulsion: geared turbines. Length 723 ft. Beam 92 ft. Gross tonnage 30,000. Speed 24 knots. Length of model 7¼ in. (Alongside is the lake steamer *Milwaukee Clipper*.) Price £3 4 6

R.M.S. MAURETANIA (old and new) (CUNARD WHITE STAR)

The old ship held the Blue Riband of the Atlantic for 22 years. The new ship was built by Cammell Laird of Birkenhead in 1938 for the London-New York service. Model (old) 6½ in. long. Price £3 4 6 (new) 7¾ in. long £3 17 0

186&187. Post-war catalogue, illustration of models.

R.M.S. ORION (ORIENT LINE)
With her sister ship *Orcades*, the first British ships to be decorated in modern style. Built by Vickers Armstrong of Barrow-in-Furness in 1935. Propulsion: geared turbines. Length 640 ft. Beam 82 ft. Gross tonnage 23,371. Speed 18 knots. Length of model 6⅝ in. Price £2 18 0

M.S. BALOERAN (ROTTERDAM LLOYD)
With her sister ship the *Dempo* were small luxury ships in the Rotterdam-Dutch East Indies service. Propulsion: Sulzer-diesel. Length 551 ft. Beam 70 ft. 4 in. Gross tonnage 17,001. Speed 18 knots. Length of model 5½ in.

M.S. ORANJE (STOOMVAART MAATSCHAPPIJ NEDERLAND-AMSTERDAM)
The largest Dutch ship in the East Indies service and the fastest motor liner in existence. Propulsion: Sulzer-diesel. Length 656 ft. Beam 83 ft. 6 in. Tonnage 20,017. Speed 26 knots. Length of model 6½ in. Price £2 18 0

EXAMPLES OF HISTORIC SHIP MODELS

THE MAYFLOWER
The ship in which the Pilgrim Fathers sailed from Plymouth to America in 1620. Scale 100 ft. to 1 in. 1¾ in. long.

A Sailing Ship of the 16th Century. Scale 100 ft. to 1 in. 2 in. long.

THE FAMOUS CUTTY SARK
Beautiful clipper built in 1870. Scale 50 ft. to 1 in. (1/600th). Length of model 4½ in.

Brunel's Pioneer Liner **GREAT EASTERN**
Built in 1858. Scale 50 ft. to 1 in. Length of model 6¾ in.

Early Atlantic Liner **S.S. CITY OF PARIS**
Built by Thomson of Clydebank in 1889. Scale 50 ft. to 1 in. Length of model 5¾ in.

188&189. Post-war catalogue, illustration of models.

THE HISTORY OF THE COMPAGNIE GÉNÉRALE TRANSATLANTIQUE IN
MODEL FORM

This interesting series of waterline models to the scale of 41 ft. to the inch
(1/500th) illustrates the progress of the French Line from the *Paris* of 1856
to the *Normandie* of 1935.

Paris (1856), *Ville de Paris* (1866), *Lafayette* (1863), *Imperatrice Eugenie*
(1865), *La Normandie* (1882), *La Gascogne* (1886), *La Touraine* (1890), *La
Provence* (1905), *France* (1910), *Paris* (1921), *Ile de France* (1926), *Lafayette*
(1929), *Champlain* (1932), *Normandie* (1935).
(Made to the order of the French Line—London).

190. Post-war catalogue, illustration of models.

191. *Bassett-Lowke plan of* ALMANZORA *as sold commercially.*

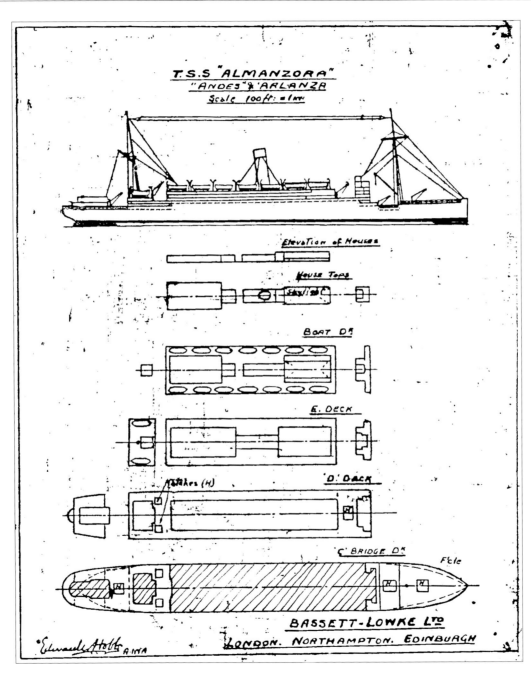

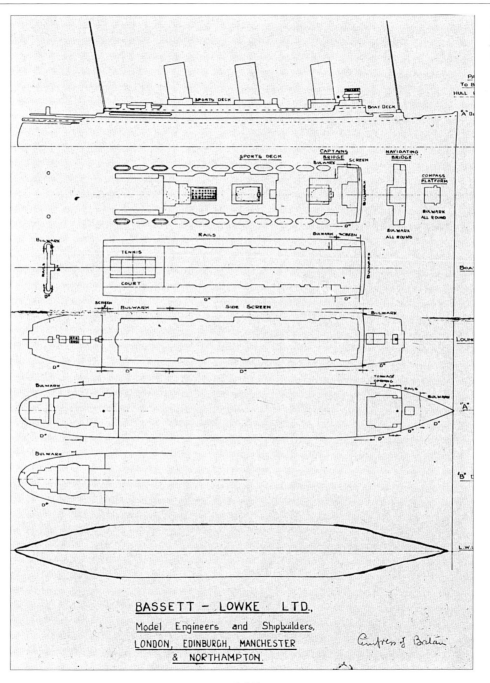

~ 50 FEET TO 1 INCH MODELS ~

Bassett-Lowke never produced anything like as wide a range of models in this larger scale as they did for the smaller one, apart from those made for the services during the war years. They were usually made to special order for individuals and, perhaps more importantly, for the shipping companies, who used them for publicity and display purposes, for instance in the windows of travel agencies.

These larger models, twice the size of their smaller counterparts, generally equalled them in terms of quality but at the same time allowed rather more detail to be included.

In 1937 Bassett-Lowke produced three kits in the 50ft. to 1in. scale representing famous ships of earlier years, namely Brunel's innovative steamer GREAT BRITAIN, his even larger and far-sighted GREAT EASTERN and the clipper ship CUTTY SARK. These retailed at

either 12/6d or 15/6d, whilst fully assembled models were priced at either 45/- or 50/-. In 1938 Cunard Line's pioneer paddle steamer Britannia was added to the range priced at 12/6d or 45/- ready assembled.

Sadly these kits were not produced after the war and as comparatively few were ever made, not many have survived to the present day. However, the 1/600th scale wartime models made for the Admiralty, consisting of all types of warship, as well as liners, cargo ships, tankers and coasters, were much more numerous and can still be found from time to time. Many have already been illustrated on pages 51 and 54-63. It is probably fortunate that fewer collectors are interested in these larger models, possibly on account of storage problems, as there are not nearly as many of them available as there are in the 1/1200th scale.

Before leaving the larger scale it is perhaps worth

193. 1/600 model of the barque ARCHIBALD RUSSELL of 1905.

194. *Contrast in size between the* QUEEN MARY *to 1/1200 and 1/600 scales.*

195. *The model of* QUEEN MARY *to 1/600 scale, in the special case supplied to the Cunard Line for publicity purposes. This particular model came from the Company's Southampton offices.*

noting that over roughly a 10-year period both before and after the last war, Bassett-Lowke built a large number of 50ft. to 1in. waterline models for Messrs. William Harvie. This old established Glasgow firm, making navigation lanterns, wished to publicise all the ships it had supplied with its products. This fine collection of models, which included merchant ships of all types, was loaned back to Bassett-Lowke for display at the Festival of Britain in 1951. The models were later sold off and although some of them are known to have been destroyed in an accident, others still exist in a private collection. Other much smaller collections to similar scales but of historic liners were also built for French Line and Union Castle and both of these were displayed for a number of years in their respective companies' office windows in the West End and City of London.

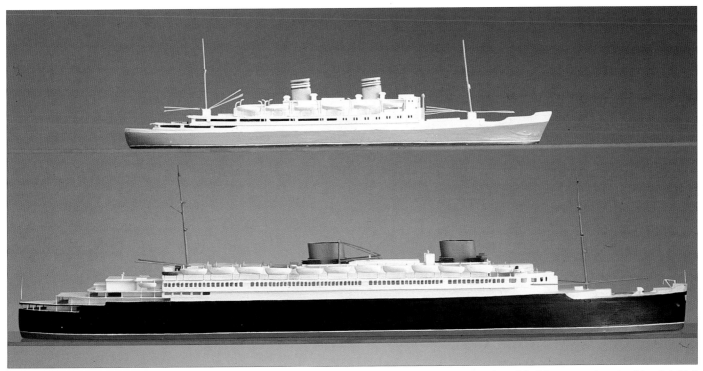

196. 1/600 models of the Norwegian liner OSLOFJORD and German liner EUROPA. The OSLOFJORD (1938) is of the Norwegian America Line. It is likely that this recognition model was made either just before, or at the start of WW2 for use by aircraft crews or submariners. She was sunk in December 1940.

197, 198&199. 1/600 models of the barque ARCHIBALD RUSSELL of 1905, the BRITANNIA (1840) and SCOT (1891).

200. The 1/600 model of SCOT, 9½ inches long.

201&202. Recognition models, 1/600 scale, of the MATHIAS-STINNES (detail at right),
the tanker ATHEL DUCHESS, and the whale factory ship, SIR JAMES CLARK ROSS.

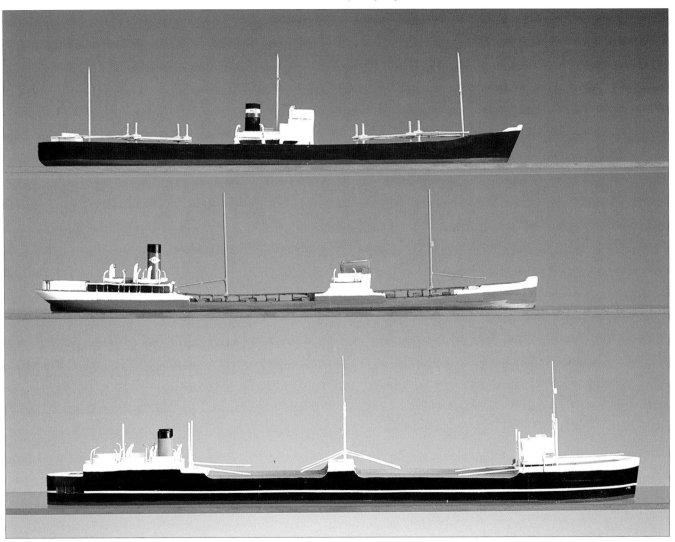

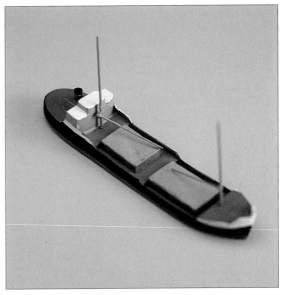

203. 1/600 model of motor coaster ARIVIAN.

204. Other 1/600 WW2 recognition models of the coaster CORHAMPTON and the Scandinavian cargo ship LOUISIANA.

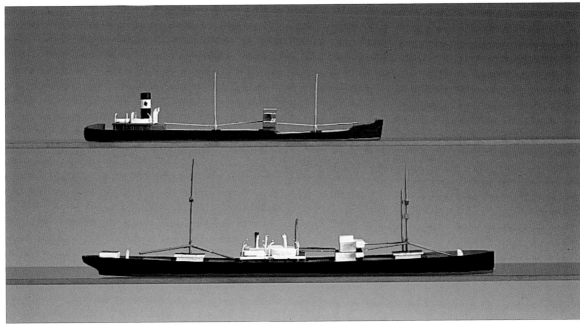

*205. The kit, scale 1/600, of the BRITANNIA which was
only available for a couple of years prior to 1940.*

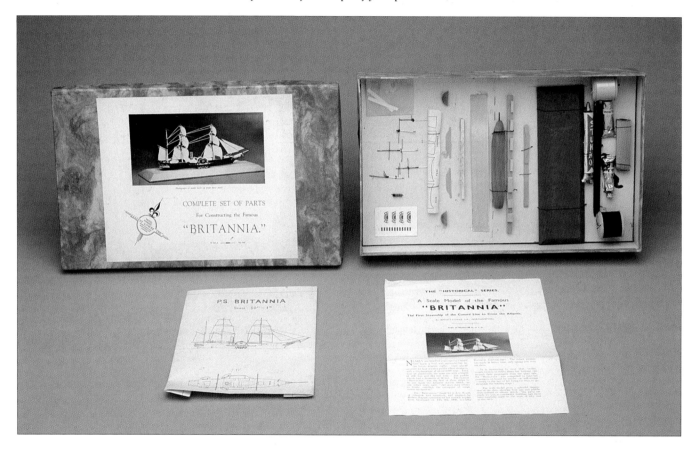

206. A photograph of Mr Harold Denton, taken in his own workshop in St Andrew's Street, Northampton in the late 1930s. He is holding a 1/600 scale model of the MONARCH OF BERMUDA, or her sister ship, with unfinished models of the MAURETANIA and ATLANTIS, at the same scale pictured in the background.

207. A pre- or post-war Bassett-Lowke label. These were stuck to the base of the model and also at the end of the individual boxes containing each model.

208. A model, scale 1/1200, of the QUEEN ELIZABETH II by the late Reginald Carpenter. Mr Carpenter, who as a Civil Servant never made models on a commercial basis, was one of the most experienced and expert model-makers to this scale since the last war.

THE PRESENT DAY

Today the collector of miniature waterline ship models, both in 1/1200th scale and even more so in the continental equivalent 1/1250th scale, has a far wider selection to choose from compared with past generations. A small diversion reviewing some of the other manufacturers would, therefore, be appropriate.

When Bassett-Lowke was at its peak in the 1930s, the only other major manufacturer of waterline ships was the large German model-making firm Wiking, which produced an extensive range of cast metal ships, both warships and merchant ships, to 1/1250th scale. These seemed somewhat crude when compared with the delicacy of Bassett-Lowke and their rather basic lifeboats, which were incorporated into the hull casting, lacked davits. Detail was fairly sparse, though the warships had trainable turrets, and windows and portholes, if shown, were represented by transfers or painting.

Sometimes the same casting, differently painted, was used for two vaguely similar ships, an example being the three-funnelled Hamburg Sud liner CAP ARCONA and the French Line PARIS. Copies of the Wiking models were also made in Denmark under the Pilot tradename.

Wiking is still in existence, marketing a wide range of high quality plastic models of road vehicles, but it has only produced a limited number of ship models since the last war, mainly in the early 1960s. Some were cast in metal, whilst others, which included the aircraft carrier USS FORRESTAL, were made of plastic and were therefore much cheaper.

In Britain there was not a lot of competition for Bassett-Lowke, certainly as far as standards went. The well known toy firm Dinky made a few liners and warships to a much smaller scale in the 1930s, but these suffered badly from metal fatigue and often broke in half.

Both before and immediately after the war, Treforest Mouldings (Tremo for short), set up by a previous employee of Wiking, produced a rather heavy-looking range of warship models in a comparatively soft metal, with the result that guns and other detail were easily snapped off. Malleable Mouldings of Deal in Kent, an early user of plastic, made a number of liners and cargo ships to 1/1200th scale, mainly for company publicity purposes, but, as mentioned earlier, these tended to warp very badly after a while, especially when removed from their wooden bases. Between 1958 and 1965 the toy manufacturer Tri-ang Minic mass produced a limited range of hard metal, 1/1200th warship and merchant ship models, along with quite an impressive number of harbour accessories. These had the advantage of being cheap and some of the castings, apart from the lifeboats which were placed on deck and not raised in davits, were rather good if lacking in detail. In the United States a firm called Superior made a wide range of medium quality warship models.

In the post-war period Germany and to a certain extent Austria have become pre-eminent in manufacturing waterline ship models to 1.1250 scale. Hansa, has produced a very large range covering all types of ship, as well as harbour accessories, while Delphin, has made a slightly cheaper range of warship models. They were soon joined by Mercator, which specialises in historic merchant ships and modern warships, and Navis/Neptun which produces detailed warship models from both World Wars. Another warship maker is Trident, based in Austria, which produced perhaps the most detailed models of all.

Over the last ten years, the list has grown still more and there is now a bewildering number of different manufacturers, mostly based in Austria and Germany. Many of them are one-man bands producing only very limited numbers of models, whilst others have several hundred in their lists, re-issuing older models from time to time if sufficient demand is forthcoming. The range of ships covered, depending on availability, is simply huge and it is not surprising that some collectors boast of collections running into the tens of thousands! With new casting techniques, quality has improved tremendously and that applies equally to those manufacturers who have chosen to work in resin, which produces beautifully crisp, if rather brittle, results. Sometimes, however, the ever-increasing emphasis on maximum detail has led to features being included that in reality

209. 1/1200 models by Mr Carpenter of the POONAH, ORIZABA, REMUERA, SERVIA, CITY OF JOHANNESBURG *and* RANGITARA.

210. Further 1/1200 models by Mr Carpenter of the CAMPANIA, LION, IXION, ARAWA, IMPERIAL STAR and DOVER. This illustrates the wide range of models made by this skilled craftsman.

would scarcely be visible to the naked eye when reduced to 1/1250th scale!

Good though these modern models are, and some, it must be admitted, are very good indeed, albeit at a price (£50 – £60 is not uncommon), in my opinion nothing can quite match the charm and excellent workmanship of Bassett-Lowke's output between 1930 and 1950.

However, mention should be made, and credit given, to three post-WW2 model-makers who specialised in the 100ft. to 1in. scale. I have over 500 ship models, both of warships and merchant ships, made by Reginald Carpenter over a period of more than 30 years. These models were produced to special orders and reflect the skill and maritime knowledge of this very talented model-maker who regrettably died in 1993. The late Leslie Osborne was another enthusiastic craftsman specialising in these small-scale replicas who made many waterline models, usually to clients' orders, for over 40 years. A third very experienced modeller is Ron Hughes, still working commercially from his home in Stowmarket, Suffolk. He has greatly extended the range of the ship models owned and enjoyed by collectors in this country and abroad. Examples of all of these three model-makers are illustrated as an addendum to this book, showing the standard and quality of their work.

Bassett-Lowke, as a company, has changed hands many times since 1950, moving its premises from one site to another, but remaining in Northampton. The most recent sale, in name only as sadly it had by then ceased trading as a model-maker, took place in the summer of 1992 and it is unlikely that any waterline models of the future will bear such an illustrious name. However, looking at the ships illustrated in this book, I hope the reader will have gained an impression of the immense skill and variety exhibited by this famous British company. The majority of the surviving models are now in private collections and it is to be hoped that their owners will continue to cherish them so that future generations may also have a chance to admire and enjoy them.

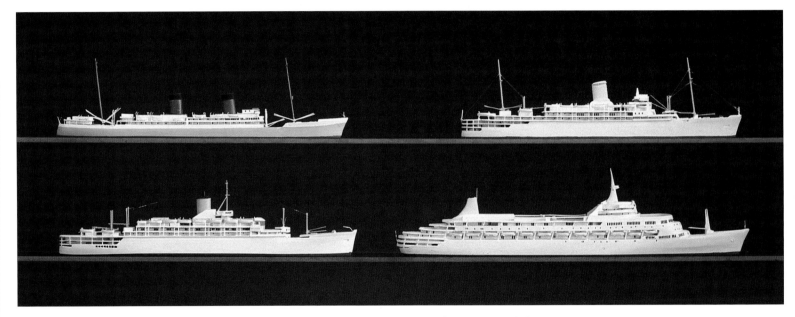

211. 1/1200 scale models by the late Leslie Osborne, including
ARUNDEL CASTLE, CHUSAN, ORCADES *and* CANBERRA. *Mr Osborne*
originally made models for Bassett-Lowke as a sub-contractor and later
made many for the public on a commercial basis.

212. 1/1200 scale models by Ron Hughes, including
LEONARDO DI VINCI, ROYAL PRINCESS, ORIANA and ROTTERDAM.
Mr Hughes is a present-day modelmaker of ships with wide experience
and expertise in this field, and with considerable knowledge of ships
and shipping.

213. Bassett-Lowke Waterline ships as promotional items. Advertisement in Shipbuilding and Shipping Record *– 1932.*

APPENDIX I.

EXTRACT FROM AN ADMIRALTY FLEET ORDER LISTING THE RECOGNITION MODELS FOR USE BY HM SHIPS OR ESTABLISHMENTS COVERING THE PRINCIPAL WARSHIPS IN SERVICE

1347.–Models of British and Foreign Warships for Instructional Purposes
(G.D. 0119/45.–15 Mar. 1945.)

The list of models contained in the Appendix to this Order is considered adequate to cover all training requirements.

2. Models are made in two sizes–50ft.to 1in., and 100ft. to 1in., <u>the former are supplied for special purposes only; the latter are to be used for all general instruction</u>.

3. Models of submarines, merchant ships and coastal craft will be supplied for new special services on their merits.

4. Fleet carriers, light fleet carriers, depot ships and establishments holding a full or partial set of models should demand new and revised models from the Director of Stores, Admiralty.

5.(a) Models marked with an asterisk are name changes to existing models and are not additional.

(b) Models marked (N) are additional to the previous order.

(c) Models marked (R) indicate a revised one is being produced.

(d) The word 'class' has been added to names in this order where *existing models* represent more than one ship.

6. Models which are replaced by a revised one or models with numbers that do not appear in the Appendix should be returned to S.N.S.O. Chatham for disposal.

7. The Rate Book for Naval stores will be amended.

APPENDIX
Models of British and Foreign War Vessels
(Pattern 1760)

British

Battleships

B.1	KING GEORGE V Class
2	MALAYA
3	ROYAL SOVEREIGN
4	NELSON
5	QUEEN ELIZABETH

Battle Cruisers

B.6	RENOWN

Aircraft Carriers

B.8	ILLUSTRIOUS Class
11	UNICORN
12	TRACKER Class (R)
51	NAIRANA (N)
52	COLOSSUS Class (N)

Cruisers

B.13	FIJI Class (3 turrets)
15	DIDO Class
53	Modified Dido Class (N)
16	SOUTHAMPTON Class (R)
17	LONDON
22	KENT Class
43	DEVONSHIRE
18	LEANDER
19	ARETHUSA
20	'D' Class
50	CALEDON (A/A Ship)

Destroyers

B.24	'L' and 'M' Classes (R)
25	'J' and 'K' Classes
26	Tribal Class
27	'H' Class
28	Packenham Class
44	'Q' and 'R' Classes
45	'S' Class (R)
30	Wairs
31	Town Class
32	Hunt Class (Type 3)
54	Weapons Class (N)
55	Battle Class (N)

Destroyer depot Ship

B.33	Tyne

Fast Minelayer

B.35	Abdiel

Monitors

B.36	Roberts

Minesweepers

B.37	Halcyon Class
38	Bangor Class
46	Algerine Class

Sloop

B.39	Modified Black Swan

Corvettes

B.40	Flower Class
41	Kingfisher Class
48	Castle Class

Frigates

B.42	River Class
47	Captain Class
49	Loch Class

American

Battleships

A.1	Maryland Class
2	Tennessee Class
3	Pennsylvania
4	Nevada
5	New York Class
6	North Carolina Class
7	South Dakota Class
26	Iowa Class
37	New Mexico (N)

Battle Cruisers

A.27	Alaska Class

Aircraft Carriers

A.28	Essex Class
8	Ranger
9	Saratoga
29	Independence Class
30	Bogue Class
34	Casablanca Class (N)

Cruisers

A.32	Baltimore Class
33	Cleveland Class
11	Brooklyn Class (R)
13	St Louis
14	New Orleans Class

15	PENSACOLA Class		14	TONE Class (R)
16	OMAHA Class		16	YUBARI
17	NORTHAMPTON Class		17	NACHI Class
10	OAKLAND Class*		18	AOBA

Destroyers

A.35	SUMNER Class (N)		J. 19	ASASHIO Class
31	FLETCHER Class		20	FUBUKI Class*
19	McCALL Class		21	MINEKAZE Class*
20	SELFRIDGE Class*		22	HATSUHARU Class
21	DRAYTON Class		23	WAKATAKE Class
23	HUGHES Class		24	SHIRATSUYU Class
24	SOMERS Class		25	KAMIKAZE Class
25	FARRAGUT Class		26	AKITSUYI Class
36	RUDDEROW Class (N)			

Italian

Japanese

Battleships

			I. 1	LITTORIO Class
J. 27	Yamato Class (N)		2	CONTE DI CAVOUR Class
1	NAGATO Class		3	DUILO Class
2	ISE Class (R)			
4	KONGO Class			

Battleships (Japanese)

Cruisers (Italian)

			I. 4	REGOLO Class
			5	ABRUZZI Class*
			6	RAIMONDO MONTECUCCLI
			7	CADORNA

Aircraft Carriers

J 5	HOSHO (R)			
7	SHOKAKU Class (R)			
28	TAIHO (N)			
29	HITAKA Class (N)			

Destroyers (Italian)

			I. 10	ORIANA Class*
			11	NAVIGATORI Class
			12	NEMBO Class
			13	SIRTORI Class
			14	DARDO Class
			15	MAESTRALE Class*

Cruisers (Japanese)

J 30	AGANO Class (N)
9	ATAGO Class
13	NATORI Class

German		French	
Battleships		*Battleships*	
G.4	ADMIRAL SCHEER	F.1	RICHELIEU
5	LUTZOW	4	BRETAGNE Class*
Cruisers		*Aircraft Carriers*	
G.7	ADMIRAL HIPPER Class	F.17	BEARN
8	KOLN	*Cruisers*	
9	NURNBERG	F.6	SUFFREN Class
10	LEIPZIG	7	La Galissoniere Class*
11	EMDEN	8	DUGUAY – TROUIN Class
Destroyers		*Destroyers*	
G.12	ELBING Class	F.10	CHACAL Class
13	NARVIK Class	11	LE FANTASQUE Class
14	LEBERCHT MAASS Class	12	BOURASQUE Class*
17	SEETIER Class	14	L'ALCYON Class
Torpedo Boats		*Sloop*	
G.15	ILTIS Class	F.16	D'ENTRESCASTEAUX
16	T.1 – T.21 Class*		

(A.F.Os 4122/43, 2395/44, 2934/44 are cancelled.)

APPENDIX II.

LIST OF WATERLINE MODELS MADE BY
MISS JUDITH HUGHES AT TAVISTOCK, DEVON
FOR BASSETT-LOWKE TO BE SUPPLIED TO THE
ROYAL NAVY AND ROYAL AIR FORCE IN WW2

Date made		Name	Number
1941	Dec.	GUARDIAN	21
1942	Jan.	Oil Tankers	10
	Feb.	COURBET	2
	"	DUNKERQUE	2
	"	EMILE BERTIN	1
	"	ALGERIE	2
	"	ITSUKUSIMA MARU (scale 50'-1")	7
	"	LA GALISSONIERE	1
	"	10,000 ton Liners (names not known)	10
	"	HANSA liners (scale 50'-1")	7
	Mar.	EIDER class (scale 50'-1")	7
	"	SIROGAUE MARU (scale 50'-1")	7
	Apr.	RAM class (scale 50'-1")	7
	"	SAKITO MARU (scale 50'-1")	7
	"	RAM class (scale 50'-1")	7
	May	PIETRO ORSELLO (scale 50'-1")	7
	"	HELGOLAND (scale 50'-1")	7
	"	DUGUAY TRURIN (scale 50'-1")	22
	"	ALGERIE	21
	Jun.	EIDER	15
	"	HOMBERG coaster	15
	Jul.	EL DJEZAIR	14
	"	COTE D'AZURE	14
	"	EHRENFELS	14
	"	RAMB	14
	Aug.	COURBET	20
	"	HYUGA	21
	"	Tribal class	20
	Sep.	DUNKERQUE	20
	Oct.	'L' class destroyers (scale 50'-1")	15
	Dec.	LEONE	1
	"	BORIA	1
	"	COURBET	9

Date made		Name	Number	Date made		Name	Number
1943	Jan.	DUNKERQUE	10	"		LITTORIA	3
	Feb.	SARATOGA	47		Jul.	NEW YORK	10
	Apr.	Italian submarines (25'-1")	35	"		NORTH CAROLINA	10
	"	" " " "	35	"		RMS QUEEN ELIZABETH	1
	"	NEW YORK	21	"		RMS QUEEN ELIZABETH	12
	"	NEW YORK (scale 50'-1")	2		Sep.	REGOLO	11
	"	SARATOGA	5		Oct.	MILWAUKEE CLIPPER (for B-L only)	2
	"	RANGER	6	"		FUSO	26
	May.	PENNSYLVANIA	4		Dec.	NAGATO	31
	"	ISE	6	"		KENT	26
	"	TRIESTE	6	"		SAN DIEGO	30
	"	VINCENZO GIOBETTI	7	1945	Jan.	ADMIRAL HIPPER	20
	Jun.	RICHELIEU	21	"		HUGHES	21
	"	PROVENCE	21		Feb.	KOGO	26
	Jul.	COURBET	20	"		DUGUAY TRURIN	20
	Sep.	RANGER	46	"		HOSO	30
1943	Oct.	SEETER	6		Apr.	NEW YORK (scale 50'-1")	1
	"	RICHELIEU	22	"		ATAGO	16
	"	CORDONA	20	"		VINCENZO GIOBERTI	25
	Nov.	EMDEN	21	"		CONTI DI CAVOUR	21
	Dec.	Wairs class destroyer	16		May.	HOSO	15
	"	NEW MEXICO	51	"		BALTIMORE	5
1944	Jan.	PACKENHAM	16	"		SOUTH DAKOTA	15
	"	BEARN	73		Jun.	FARRAGUT (scale 50'-1")	1
	Feb.	ILLUSTRIOUS	21	"		HUGHES (scale 50'-1")	1
	"	Hunt class destroyer	16	"		NORTH CAROLINA	15
	Mar.	LCI(S) (25'-1")	30	"		REGOLO	20
	"	RANGER	40		Jul.	ESSEX	6
	May.	TYNE	13	"		HUGHES	15
	"	KING GEORGE V	3	"		FARRAGUT	11
	"	MARAT	3		Sep.	HYUGA	106
	"	TIRPITZ	3		Oct.	RMS QUEEN ELIZABETH	12
				"		SOUTH DAKOTA	6

Date made		Name	Number
	Nov.	NORTH CAROLINA	6
	"	RMS QUEEN ELIZABETH	1
	Dec.	EXETER	1
1946	Feb.	SOUTH DAKOTA	9
	"	SARATOGA	14
	"	RANGER	4
	Mar.	NEVADA	14
	"	MARYLAND	10
	Apr.	TENNESSEE	9
	Jul.	COLOSSUS (scale 50'-1")	1
	"	SOUTH DAKOTA (scale 50'-1")	1
	Sep.	NEVADA (scale 50'-1")	1
	"	TENNESSEE (scale 50'-1")	1
	"	MARYLAND (scale 50'-1")	1
	"	HUGHES (scale 50'-1")	1
	Oct.	ESSEX (scale 50'-1")	1
	"	SOMERS (scale 50'-1")	1
	"	NORTH CAROLINA (scale 50'-1")	1
	Nov.	SOUTH DAKOTA (scale 50'-1")	1
	"	IOWA (scale 50'-1")	1
1947	Jan.	RMS QUEEN ELIZABETH (for B-L) (all to scale of 50'-1")	7
	Mar.	CAIRO (scale 50'-1")	1
	Apr.	CLEOPATRA (scale 50'-1")	1
	May.	RMS QUEEN ELIZABETH (for B-L)	10
	Sep.	IOWA (scale 50'-1")	2
	"	DIDO (scale 50'-1")	2
	"	CASABLANCA (scale 50'-1")	2
	"	FIJI (scale 50'-1")	2
1948	Jan.	RMS QUEEN ELIZABETH (for B-L)	12
	Feb.	RMS QUEEN MARY (for B-L)	12
	Aug.	SOUTH DAKOTA	10
	Nov.	KING GEORGE V (for B-L)	11

Date made		Name	Number
1950	Apr.	SS ILE DE FRANCE (for B-L)	29
	May.	SS ILE DE FRANCE (for B-L)	31
	Sep.	RMS ORCADES (for B-L)	4

1951 One model of L.C.M. was made to ¼" scale for the School of Combined Operations at Fremington.

All the above models were to a scale of 100ft. to 1in. unless otherwise stated.

APPENDIX III.

A LIST OF ROYAL NAVAL RECOGNITION MODELS, SCALE 50'–1", CIRCA 1955, WHICH WERE THE FINAL ONES ISSUED TO THIS SCALE

Number

M.1.L	WILLIAM RUYS	Dutch Liner
M.2.L	URUGUAY STAR	British Cargo Liner
M.3.L	PORTLAND STAR	British Cargo Liner
M.4.L	CITY OF BIRMINGHAM	British Cargo Liner
M.5.L	BRULLOYNE	Cargo Ship
M.6.L	GRAINTON	British Cargo Ship
M.7.L	TRELISSICK	British Cargo Ship
M.8.L	CABOSILLIERO	Spanish Cargo Ship
M.9.L	BRITISH FERN	British Tanker
M.10.L	DUBRECA	French Fruit Carrier
M.11.L	OCEAN COAST	British Coastal Ship
M.12.L	FALLAISE	BritishCross-Channel Ship

The details of these models were contained in an Admiralty Order dated 1954, and they were available for instruction from that time, to Naval Establishments.

**A LIST OF ROYAL NAVAL POST-WAR
RECOGNITION MODELS, MADE BETWEEN 1946
AND 1975, SOME OF WHICH WERE PRODUCED
BY BASSETT-LOWKE. THESE WERE THE FINAL
MODELS USED BY THE ROYAL NAVY AND WERE
WITHDRAWN IN 1984**

*Class/Group/
Pattern Number*

0691-461-11023	BRITISH FERN	British Tanker
11085	COMMENCEMENT BAY	USA A/C
11096	FARGO	USA Cruiser
11100	SUMNER	USA Destroyer
11127	KIROV	Russian Cruiser
11134	GORDY	Russian Destroyer
11139	PULUKHIN	Russian Sweeper
4413	TIGER	British Cruiser
4414	'Q' class	Russian Submarine
4415	'A' class	British Submarine
4416	DON	Russian D/S
4417	ANDIZHAN	Russian D/S
4418	KUBAN	Russian D/S
4419	SOLDEK	Russian D/S
4420	CHULYM	Russian D/S
4421	DONBASS	Russian D/S
4422	ATREK	Russian D/S
4423	'F' class	Russian Submarine
4424	'Z' class	Russian Submarine
4425	'W' class	Russian Submarine
4426	'Q' class	Russian Submarine
4427	FORREST SHERMAN	USA Destroyer
4428	MITSCHER	USA Destroyer
4429	FORRESTAL	USA A/C
4431	OCEAN COAST	UK Cargo Ship
4432	CITY OF BIRMINGHAM	UK Cargo Liner
4433	WILLEM RUYS	Dutch Liner
4434	DUBREKA	French Cargo Ship
4443	BALTIMORE	USA Cruiser
4444	SALEM	USA Cruiser
4445	ARK ROYAL	UK A/C
4446	CEYLON	UK Cruiser
4447	DARING	UK Destroyer
4448	BLACKWOOD	UK Frigate
4449	ROCKET	UK Frigate
4450	ST LAURENT	Canadian Frigate
4451	DE RUYTER	Dutch Cruiser
4452	HOLLAND	Dutch Destroyer
4453	CHAPAEV	Russian Cruiser
4455	KOTLIN	Russian Destroyer
4456	SKORY	Russian Destroyer
4457	KOLA	Russian Destroyer
4483	WHITBY	UK Frigate

APPENDIX IV.

MODELS OF LINERS ADDED OR OMITTED TO THE BASSETT-LOWKE CATALOGUES BETWEEN 1929 AND 1939

Added	Omitted
1930	
EMPRESS OF BRITAIN CPR	COLUMBUS N.GermanLloyd
FRANCE French Line	AUGUSTUS Nav.G.T.
ORFORD Orient Line	ANDES R.M.S.P.
ARLANDA R.M.S.P.	
VULCANIA Colusich Line	
1931	
BREMEN N.German Lloyd	CELTIC White star Line
EUROPA	
LAFAYETTE Cie. G.T.	
EMPRESS OF JAPAN C.P.R.	
VICEROY OF INDIA P.&O.	
WINCHESTER CASTLE Union Castle	
ATLANTIS R.M.S.P.	
1932	
CHAMPLAIN Cie. G.T.	CEDRIC White Star Line
STRATHNAVER P.&O.	ARAGUAYA R.M.S.P.
STRATHAIRD P.&O.	DORIC White Star Line
WARWICK CASTLE	
Union Castle	PITTSBURG ”
ORMOND Orient Line	
1933	
REX Italian Line	
MANHATTAN United States Line	
WASHINGTON United States Line	
L'ATLANTIQUE C.de N. Sud-Atlantique	
EMPRESS OF CANADA C.P.R.	
BERMUDA Furness Withy Line	
QUEEN OF BERMUDA Furness Withy Line	
CAP ARCONA Hamburg S.A. Line	
BRITANNIC White Star Line	
HIGHLAND CHIEFTAIN Royal Mail	
CARIBIA Hamburg America Line	

Added	Omitted
1934	
NORMANDIE French Line	
DEMPO Rotterdam Lloyd Line	
BALOERAN Rotterdam Lloyd Line	
1935	
ORION Orient Line	AVILA STAR Blue Star Line
SCHARNHORST N. German Lloyd	
	AVELONA STARBlue Star Line
	ANDALUCIA STAR " "
	CALGARIC " "
	REGINA " " "
	ALBERTIC " " "
	BELGENLAND Red Star Line
1936	
QUEEN MARY Cunard	EMPRESS OF SCOTLAND C.P.R
CHICHIBU MARU N.Y.K.	BALTIC White star Line
STRATHMORE P.& O.	ARCADIAN Royal Mail
AWATEA U.S.Co. of N.Z.	FRANCE French Line
STIRLING CASTLE Union Castle	
	ALBERT BALLIN
	Hamburg-Amerika
ATHELONE CASTLE Union Castle	
PRINCE BAUDOUIN Belgium State	
1937	
PRETORIA German-Africa Line	
WINDHUK German-Africa Line	
1938	
CONTE DI SAVOIA Italian Line	
COLOMBIE French Line	
NIEUW AMSTERDAM Holland-America Line	
CAPETOWN CASTLE Union Castle	
ORCADES Orient Line	
MONARCH OF BERMUDA Furness Withy Line	
EMPRESS OF SCOTLAND C.P.R. (Re-introduced)	

Added	Omitted
MONTCLARE C.P.R.	
MONTROSE C.P.R.	
VICTORIA Lloyd Triestino Line	
COLOMBIA Royal Netherlands	
ALBERTIC (incorrectly listed as Royal Mail)	
1939/1940	
New MAURETANIA Cunard	
	MINNETONKA
	Atlantic Transport
DOMINION MONARCH Shaw Savill	
	HILDEBRAND
	Booth Steamship Co.
	ALBERTIC
	shown as Royal Mail

APPENDIX V.

LIST OF KNOWN MODELS MADE BY BASSETT-LOWKE TO 100ft. to 1in. SCALE

WW1 – WARSHIPS

BRITISH

Battleships: MAJESTIC class, CANOPUS class, LONDON class, KING EDWARD VII class, DREADNOUGHT, ST VINCENT class, SWIFTSURE, LORD NELSON, THUNDERER, BELLEROPHON class, NEPTUNE, COLOSSUS class, AGINCOURT, ORION class, KING GEORGE V class, IRON DUKE class, QUEEN ELIZABETH class and ROYAL SOVEREIGN class.

Battle Cruisers: INVINCIPLE class, NEW ZEALAND class, LION class, TIGER, REPULSE, RENOWN and GLORIOUS class.

Aircraft Carriers: FURIOUS, ENGADINE.

Cruisers: CRESSY class, DRAKE class, MONMOUTH class, DEVONSHIRE class, WARRIOR class, MINOTOUR class, EDGAR class, HIGHFLYER class, DIADEM class, PELORUS class, FORWARD class, GLASGOW class, DARTMOUTH class, ARETUSA class, SOUTHAMPTON class, CAMBRIAN class, CAROLINE class.

Destroyers: ACORN, ALARM, ALBACORE, BRISK, BONETTA, BOYNE, BADGER, DERWENT, DOON, BOXER, LURCHER, OAK, KALE, KANGAROO, FIREDRAKE, MYRMIDON, SHELDRAKE, Torpedo Boats Nos 10, 11& 12.

Submarines: A3, 4, 5&6; B1, 2, 4&5; C1&2; E1, 2&3.

Royal Yachts: ENCHANTRESS & VICTORIA&ALBERT.

Hospital Ship: MAINE.

Troopship: INDIA.

Repair Ship: COCHRANE.

FRANCE

Battleships: MASSINA, DEMOCRATIE, JUSTICE, VERITÉ.

Dreadnoughts & Battle Cruisers: NORMANDIE, GASCOYNE, LANGUEDOC, FLANDRES, BEARNE, BRETAGNE, LORRAINE, PROVENCE, COURBET, JEAN BART, PARIS, FRANCE, DANTON, MIRABEAN, DIDEROT, CONDORCET, VERNIAND, VOLTAIRE.

Cruisers: CONDÉ, VICTOR HUGO, JULES FERRY, ERNEST RENAN, EDGAR QUINET, GLOIRE.

Destroyers: FOURCHÉ, BORY, CASQUE.

GERMANY

Battleships: DEUTSCHLAND, HANNOVER, POMMERN, SCHLESWIG-HOLSTEIN, SCHLESIE.

Dreadnoughts & Battle Cruisers: GROSSE KURFURST, KRONPRINZ, KOENIG, MARKGRAF, KAISER, FREDRICH DER GROSSE, KAISERIN, PRINZ REGENT LUITPOLD, KONIG ALBERT, THURINGEN, HELGOLAND, OSTERIESLAND, OLDENBURG, DERFFLINGER, LUTZOW, ERSATZ HERTHA, SEYDLITZ, MOLKE, GOEBEN, VON DER TANN.

Cruisers: EMDEN, BRESLAU, STRALSUND, STRASSBURG, MAGDEBURG, BERLIN, KONIGSBERG, STETTIN, DRESDEN, ELBING, FRANKFURT.

Destroyers: T, G, S & V CLASS.

USA

Battleships: KANSAS, VERMONT, NEW HAMPSHIRE, MINNESOTA, IDAHO, NEVADA, TEXAS, ARKANSAS, UTAH.

Cruisers: NORTH CAROLINA, MONTANA, WASHINGTON, TENNESSEE, COLORADO, ST LOUIS.

AUSTRIA/HUNGARY

Battleships: ERZHERZOG KARL, FRANZ FERDINAND, ZRINZI, RADETZKY.

Dreadnoughts & Battle Cruisers: VIRIBUS UNIBUS, TEGETTHOF, P. EUGEN, SZENT ISTRAV.
Cruisers: SAIDA, HELGOLAND, NOVARA, SANKT GEORG.
Destroyers: TATRA, ULAN, MAGNET.

ITALY
Battleships: PISA, AMALFIN, SAN GIORGIO, SAN MARCO, CONTE DI CAVOUR.
Cruisers: QUARTO, LIBIA, PUGLIA.
Destroyers: COATIT, MINERVA.

RUSSIA
Battleships: IMPERATOR PAVAL, ANDREI PERVOSIVAMI, RURIK.
Dreadnoughts & Battle Cruisers: GANGOOT, POLTAVA, PETROPARLOVSK, SEVASTOPOL, IMPERATOR ALEXANDRE III.
Cruisers: RURIK, ADMIRAL MAKAROFF, BAYAN.
Destroyers: SCHICHAU, NORMAD, STRASHNI.

JAPAN
Battleships: KASTUMA, KATORI, KONGO, FUSO, AKI.
Cruisers: NISSHIN, KASUGA, AZUMA, YAKUMO, ASO.
Destroyers: SAKURA, ARARE, OBORO.

WW1 – LINERS

Cunard Line: AQUITANIA, MAURETANIA, LUSITANIA.
White Star Line: OLYMPIC, TITANIA.
Hamburg-American Line: IMPERATOR, VATERLAND.
Compagnie General Translantique: FRANCE.
North German Lloyd: KRONPRINZESSIN CECILIE, KAISER WILHELM II.
Union Castle Line: BALMORAL CASTLE, EDINBURGH CASTLE.
Hamburg-American Line: CAP TRAFALGAR, CAP POLONIO.
Canadian Pacific Line: EMPRESS OF ASIA, EMPRESS OF RUSSIA.
Royal Mail Line: ASTURIAS, AMAZON.
American Line: ST LOUIS, ST PAUL.
Orient Line: OTRANTO.
P&O Line: MACEDONIA, MARMORA, MOLDAVIA, MONGOLIA.
Royal Holland S.S.Co: GELRIA, TURBANTIA.
Booth S.S.Co: HILARY.
Viking Cruising Co: VIKING (Ex. ATRATO).
S.E.&C. Railway Co: ENGADINE, RIVIERA.
Dover & Ostend S.S.Co: VILLE DE LIEGE.

WARSHIP MODELS SOLD COMMERCIALLY BETWEEN 1922-1940 (excluding those made to special order)

BRITISH
Battleships: KING GEORGE V class, IRON DUKE class, ERIN, QUEEN ELIZABETH class, NELSON, RODNEY.
Battle Cruisers: TIGER, LION, RENOWN, REPULSE, HOOD.
Aircraft Carriers: COURAGEOUS, GLORIOUS, FURIOUS.
Cruisers: ARETHUSA class, CAMBRIAN class, CALEDON class, HAWKINS class, YORK, ENTERPRISE, LONDON class, LEANDER class.
Destroyers: SPENCER, V&W class, SWIFT, ANZAC, AMBUSCADE.
Submarines: L&M classes, X1.
Minesweeper: HUNT class.
China Station Gun Boats: INSECT class (Bee).
Oil Tankers: BURMA, PETROLEUM.
Monitor: TERROR.
Submarine Depot Ship: TITANIA.

GERMANY
Pocket Battleship: ERSATZ PREUSSEN (DEUTSCHLAND).

RECOGNITION MODELS WW2

BRITAIN AND COMMONWEALTH

Battleships: VALIANT, MALAYA, BARHAM, REVENGE, ROYAL SOVEREIGN, RESOLUTION, RAMILLES, NELSON, KING GEORGE V (1941), KING GEORGE V (1944).

Battle Cruisers: HOOD, REPULSE, RENOWN (1942), RENOWN (1947).

Aircraft Carriers: FURIOUS (1938), FURIOUS (1941), EAGLE, HERMES, ARGUS, COURAGEOUS, GLORIOUS, ARK ROYAL, ILLUSTRIOUS, INDOMITABLE, UNICORN, IMPLACABLE, OCEAN, ARCHER, TRACKER, ATTACKER, NAIRANA, ALBATROSS.

Monitor: ROBERTS.

Cruisers: LONDON, DEVONSHIRE, KENT (1939), KENT (1941), NORFOLK, CUMBERLAND, BERWICK, CORNWALL, HAWKINS, EFFINGHAM, YORK, EXETER (1938), EXETER (1941), DORSETSHIRE, SOUTHAMPTON (1938), GLASGOW (1945), BELFAST, FIJI, UGANDA, BERMUDA, ARETHUSA (1939), ARETHUSA (1942), ARETHUSA (1944), GALATEA, DIDO, SIRIUS, EURYALUS, DIADEM, HOBART, ADELADE, ORION, NEPTUNE, LEANDER (1946), AMPHIAN, CALEDON (1938),CALEDON (1940), CALYPSO, CAPETOWN, COLOMBO, CALCUTTA, CARLISLE (1941), COVENTRY (1940), DANAE, DAUNTLESS, DELHI (1942), EMERALD (1939), EMERALD (1941), ENTERPRISE.

Mine-Laying Cruisers: ADVENTURE (1939), ADVENTURE (1941), ABDIEL.

Destroyers: SKATE, SABRE, WALLACE, WILD SWAN, WINCHESTER, WISHART, VEGA, AMAZON, AMBUSCADE, ACHATES, GRAFTON, EXPRESS, ECLIPSE, AFRIDI, JANUS, JAVELIN, MILNE, TEAZER, HASTY, ONSLOW, PENN, TYRIAN, URANIA, CAVALIER, CAVENDISH, BARFLEUR, BRIGHTON, GORE, ATHERSTON, BEAUFORT, BLEASDALE.

Sloops and Frigates: LEITH, GRIMSBY, SHOREHAM, FLEETWOOD, EGRET, PELICAN, TAFF, LOCH DUNREGAN, MOUNTS BAY, SNIPE.

Minesweepers: HALCYON, BANGOR, RATTLESNAKE.

Corvettes: KINGFISHER, ABELIA, VETCH, FLINT CASTLE.

Submarines: CLYDE (1938), SEVERN (1940), THAMES (1937), PORPOISE, SEALION, TRIBUNE, ANDREW, CACHELOT.

Support Ships: TYNE, MAIDSTONE, MEDWAY, GUARDIAN.

USA

Battleships: NEW YORK, NEVADA, ARIZONA, ARKANSAS, PENNSYLVANIA (1937), PENNSYLVANIA (1942), NEW MEXICO (1938), NEW MEXICO (1942), MISSISSIPPI (1938), IDAHO (1940), TENNESSEE (1940), TENNESSEE (1944), WEST VIRGINIA (1940), MARYLAND (1940), MARYLAND (1944), COLORADO (1940), SOUTH DAKOTA (1943), WASHINGTON, IOWA.

Battle Cruisers: ALASKA.

Aircraft Carries: LEXINGTON (1938), SARATOGA (1942), RANGER, YORKTOWN, ESSEX, BOGUE, COMMENCENT BAY, CASABLANCA, LANGLEY, CHARGER.

Cruisers: OMAHA, PENSACOLA (1939), PENSACOLA (1944), SALT LAKE CITY (1939), SALT LAKE CITY (1941), PORTLAND (1939), INDIANAPOLIS (1938), CHESTER (1941), AUGUSTA (1941), LOUISVILLE (1945), NEW ORLEANS (1941), BROOKLYN, PHILADELPHIA, ST LOUIS, WICHITA, BALTIMORE, ATLANTA.

Destroyers: BORIE, CRANE, FARRAGUT, MAURY, McCALL, SELFRIDGE, DRAYTON, HUGHES, SOMERS, FLETCHER, RUDDEROW.

Auxiliaries: TERROR, DIXIE.

FRANCE

Battleships: COURBET, PROVENCE, BRETAGNE, DUNKERQUE, RICHELIEU.

Aircraft Carriers: BEARN (1943), BEARN (1945).
Seaplane Carrier: COMMANDANT TESTE.
Cruisers: DUGUAY-TROUIN, TOURVILLE, SUFFREN, FOCH, DUPLEIX, JEANNE-D'ARC, ALGERIE, EMILE BERTIN, LA GALISSONNIÈRE, LA TOUR D'AUVERGNE (PLUTON).
Destroyers: SIMOUN, L'ALCYON, GUEPARD, AIGLE, LE FANTASQUE, BRANLEBAS, BOURRASQUE.
Sloop: D'ENTRECASTEAUX.
Submarines: SURCOUF, REQUIN, REDOUTABLE.

HOLLAND
Cruisers: SUMATRA, TROMP, DE RUYTER.

GERMANY
Battleships: ADMIRAL GRAF SPEE, DEUTSCHLAND, ADMIRAL SHEER, GNEISENAU, SCHARNHORST, BISMARCK, TIRPITZ, LUTZOW.
Cruisers: EMDEN, KOHN, NURNBERG, LEIPZIG, ADMIRAL HIPPER, PRINZ EUGEN.
Destroyers: WOLF, LEBERECHT MAASS, KARL GALSTER, NARVIK class, SEETIER, T.18.
Submarines: U.7 (type IIB), U.65 (type IXB), U.94 (type VII), U.317 (type VIID).
Minesweeper: M.7.

ITALY
Battleships: CONTE DI CAVOUR, ANDREA DORIA, LITTORIO.
Cruisers: BARI, TRESTE, ALBERTO DI GIUSSANO, BARTOLOMEO COLLEONI, ARMANDO DIAZ, LUIGI CADORNA, BOLZANO, RAIMONDO MONTECUCCOLI, LUIGI DI SAVOIA, GIUSEPPE GARABALDI, REGOLO, POLA, ZARA.
Destroyers: G. SIRTORI, LEONE, BOREA, LUCA TARIGO (Navigatori class), BALENO, DARDO, GRECALE (Maestrale class), ALFREDO ORIANI, MAESTRALE.
Submarines: BALILLA, FERRARIS, ATROPO, NANI.

JAPAN
Battleships: HARUNA, FUSO, MUTSO, NAGATO, ISE (1940), ISE (1945), HYUGA (1942), HYUGA (1945), KONGO, YAMATO.
Aircraft Carriers: HOSHO, SHOKAKU, SORU, RYUZYO, KAGA, TAIHO, HITAKA.
Cruisers: NATORI, KINUGASA, SENAI, MAYA, KAKO, NATI (NACHI), TAKAO, ATAGO, AGANO, YUBARI, TONE, AOBA (1945), KATORI, MOGAMI, TENRYU, KUMA.
Destroyers: MOMI, KAGERO, SIRAKUMU, TERUTSUKI, ASASHIU, FUBUKI, MINEKAZE, HATSUHARU, WAKATAKE (1944), SHIRATSUYU, KAMIKAZE, AKITSUKI.
Seaplane Carrier: CHITOSE.

RUSSIA
Battleship: MARAT.
Cruisers: KRASNI KAUKAZ, MAXIM GORKI, CHAPAEV.
Destroyers: LENINGRAD, GORDI, STROGI, SHAUYAN.

MERCHANT SHIPS, LINERS AND CARGO VESSELS PRODUCED BETWEEN 1925 AND 1966

Cunard Line: CARMANIA, CARONIA, SAMARIA, FRANCONIA (black & white hull), SCYTHIA, ANTONIA, ASCANIA, ALAUNIA, AUSONIA, MAURETANIA (black & white hull), MAURETANIA (hospital ship), AQUITANIA, AQUITANIA (hospital ship), BERENGARIA, QUEEN MARY, new MAURETANIA, QUEEN ELIZABETH, QUEEN ELIZABETH (troop ship), QUEEN ELIZABETH (1952 version), CARINTHIA, CARONIA (1948).
White Star Line: OLYMPIC, TITANIC, ADRIATIC, BALTIC, CEDRIC, CELTIC, HOMERIC, LAURENTIC, ALBERTIC, DORIC, CALGARIC, PITTSBURG, CERAMIC, REGINA, MAJESTIC, BRITANNIC, GEORGIC, GEORGIC (1949).

Canadian Pacific Railway S.S. Co: EMPRESS OF ASIA, EMPRESS OF RUSSIA, EMPRESS OF SCOTLAND (black & white hulls), EMPRESS OF FRANCE, EMPRESS OF AUSTRALIA, EMPRESS OF JAPAN, EMPRESS OF BRITAIN, DUCHESS OF ATHOLL, DUCHESS OF RICHMOND, DUCHESS OF BEDFORD, DUCHESS OF YORK, MONTCLARE, MONTCALM, MONTROSE, PRINCESS MARGUERITE.

P&O: NALDERA, NARKUNDA, MOOLTAN, MALOJA, MONGOLIA, RANCHI, VICEROY OF INDIA, RANCHI (1947), STRATHAIRD, STRATHAIRD (1948), STRATHNAVER, STRATHNAVER (1948).

Orient Line: OTRANTO, ORMOND, ORANIA, ORONSAY, ORFORD, ORION, ORCADES, ORCADES (1950).

Red Star Line: PENNLAND, BELGENLAND, PITTSBURG, WESTERLAND.

Booth Line: HILARY, HILDEBRAND.

Union Castle Line: BALMORAL CASTLE, EDINBURGH CASTLE, WINDSOR CASTLE, ARUNDEL CASTLE, CARNAVON CASTLE, WINCHESTER CASTLE, STIRLING CASTLE, ATHELON CASTLE, CAPE TOWN CASTLE.

Blue Star Line: ALMEDA STAR, AVILA STAR, AVELONA STAR, ANDALUSIA STAR, ARANDORA STAR (black hull), ARANDORA STAR (white hull 1930), ARANDORA STAR (1932), ARANDORA STAR (1935).

Royal Mail Line: ASTURIAS (1906), AMAZON, ALMANZORA, ARCADIAN, AVON, ANDES, ARAGUAYA, ARLANZA, ATLANTIS (black hull 1929), ATLANTIS (white hull 1930), ATLANTIS (hospital ship), OHIO, ASTURIAS (1926), ASTURIAS (1935), ASTURIAS (1947), ALCANTARA (1926), ALCANTARA (1935), HIGHLAND CHIEFTAIN, ANDES (1947), AMAZON (1959).

New Zealand Shipping Co: RANGITOTO (1949).

Shaw Savill Line: DOMINION MONARCH, NEW AUSTRALIA (1949).

Union Steamship Co. of New Zealand: AWATEA.

Blue Funnel Line: GLAUCUS.

Furness, Withy Line: BERMUDA, MONARCH OF BERMUDA, QUEEN OF BERMUDA, OCEAN MONARCH (1951).

Pacific Steam Nav. Co: ORBITA, ORDUNA.

Lambert Holt: VANDYCK, VOLTAIRE.

Anchor Line: BRITANNIA (1926), CALEDONIA (1925), CALIFORNIA (1923).

Aberdeen Line: MILTIADES (1903).

Australian Steamships Ltd: CANBERRA (1913).

Atlantic Transport Line: MINNETONKA.

Canadian National S.S. Co: LADY NELSON class.

United States Line: LEVIATHAN, MANHATTAN, WASHINGTON, AMERICA, UNITED STATES (1952).

Wisconsin & Michigan S.S. Co: MILWAUKEE CLIPPER.

Matson Line: MARIPOSA, MONTEREY.

French Line: FRANCE, PARIS, ILE DE FRANCE, LAFAYETTE, COLOMBIE (1931), COLOMBIE (1948), CHAMPLAIN, NORMANDIE (1935), NORMANDIE (1937), LIBERTÉ (1950), ILE DE FRANCE (2 funnels 1950).

Fraissinet CdeN: ISLE DE BEAUTÉ.

Compagnie Sud-Atlantique: MASSILA, L'ATLANTIQUE, PASTEUR.

Messageries Maritime: ARAMIS, GEORGES PHILIPPAR.

Mixte, Compagnie de Nav: EL KATARA, EL-DJEZAIR.

North German Lloyd: COLUMBUS (1922), COLUMBUS (1929), GENERAL VON STEUBEN, EUROPA (1930), EUROPA (1933), BREMEN (1929), BREMEN (1933), SCHARNHORST, GNEISENAU, EIDER, ULM, HELGOLAND.

Hamburg-America Line: RESOLUTE, RELIANCE, NEW YORK, HAMBURG, ALBERT BALLIN, ST LOUIS, MILWAUKEE, CARIBIA.

Hamburg Sud-America Line: CAP ARCONA.

German-Africa Line: PRETORIA, WINDHUK.

Hansa-Deutsche DG: REICHENFELS.

Franz Haniel: HAMBURG.

Italian Line: REX, CONTE DI SAVOIA.
Cosulich Line: SATURNIA, VULCANIA.
Navigazione Generale Italiana: AUGUSTUS.
Gdynia-America Line: PILSUDSKI.
Lloyd Triesto: VICTORIA.
Holland-America: STATENDAM, NIEUW AMSTERDAM.
Rotterdam Lloyd: DEMPO, BALOERAN.
Royal Netherlands Line: COLOMBIA.
N.Y.K: CHICHIBU MARU.
Nederland-Amsterdam: ORANJE.
Southern Railway: ENGADINE, RIVIERA, ISLE OF THANET, LORINA, BIARRITZ, NORMANIA, HANTONIA, ISLE OF GUERNSEY, ISLE OF JERSEY, ISLE OF SARK, MAID OF ORLEANS, MAID OF KENT, WORTHING, DINARD, BRITTANY, ST BRIAC, TWICKENHAM FERRY.
LMS: CAMBRIA, HIBERNIA.
LNER: VIENNA, BRUSSELS, MALINES, ANTWERP.
Belgium state Railways: VILLE DE LIEGE, JEAN BREYDELL, STADT ANTWERPEN, PIETER DE CONNICK, PRINCE BAUDOUIN.
Gérance et d'Armement: CÔTE D'AZUR.
R.A.M.B: RAMB I.
Osaka: SIROGANE MARU.
N.Y.K: SAKITO MARU, HOKOKU MARU.
Recognition models: BEN READ, ESSO FORMOSA, ATHELDUCHESS, D.L. HARPER, SIR JAMES CLARK ROSS, ARIVAIN, PIETRO ORSELLO, EHRENFELS, LOUISIANNA, DUNKFELD, MATHIAS-STINNES, MARQUIS, CAPE HAWKE, JESSMORE, MORMACPORT C3.
Dundee, Perth & London S. Co: LONDON.
Liverpool & Noth Wales S.S. Co: ST TRUDO.
Belfast S. Co: ULSTER MONARCH.
P.& A. Campbell: GLEN GOWER.
Townsend Ferries: FREE ENTERPRISE I, FREE ENTERPRISE II.
British Tankers (BP): BRITISH FAME.

Early Sailing & Steam Ships: CUTTY SARK, GREAT BRITAIN, GREAT EASTERN, BRITANNIA, GREAT WESTERN, CITY OF PARIS, PRUSSEN.
National Steamship Co: AMERICA (1884).

POST WW2 WARSHIP MODELS SOLD COMMERCIALLY FROM 1947-1950

BRITISH
Battleships and Battle Cruisers: KING GEORGE V, NELSON, QUEEN ELIZABETH, RENOWN.
Aircraft Carrier: ILLUSTRIOUS.
Cruisers: FIJI, DIDO, SOUTHAMPTON, LONDON, KENT, ARETHUSA.
Destroyers: COSSACK, CASTLE class, RIVER class, HUNT class.

USA
Battleships & Battle Cruiser: NORTH CAROLINA, MARYLAND, ALASKA.
Aircraft Carrier: SARATOGA.
Cruisers: BALTIMORE, NEW ORLEANS, AUGUSTA.

FRANCE
Battleship: RICHELIEU.
Cruisers: LA GALISSONNIÈRE, MONTCALM.

ITALY
Battleships: ITALIA, CONTE DI CAVOUR.
Cruisers: LUIGI CADORNA, BOLZANO, GIUSEPPE GARIBALDI.

GERMANY
Battleships: TIRPITZ, BISMARCK.
Cruisers: ADMIRAL HIPPER, LIEPZIG.

214. *E.S. Normandie from the* Bassett-Lowke Catalogue of Model Ships – May 1938.

INDEX

ABBREVIATIONS – NAVAL VESSELS

HMS   Royal Navy, Great Britain
FN   French Navy
IGN&GN German Navy
IJN   Japanese Navy
IN   Italian Navy
USN   United States of America Navy

ABBREVIATIONS – MERCHANT SHIPPING COMPANIES

BR   British Railways
CGT   Compagnie Genérale Transatlantique
CPR   Canadian Pacific Railways
LNER   London & North Eastern Railway
LMS   London, Midland & Scottish Railway
NYK   Nippon Yusen KK, Tokyo
P&O   Pacific & Orient Line
SR   Southern Railway

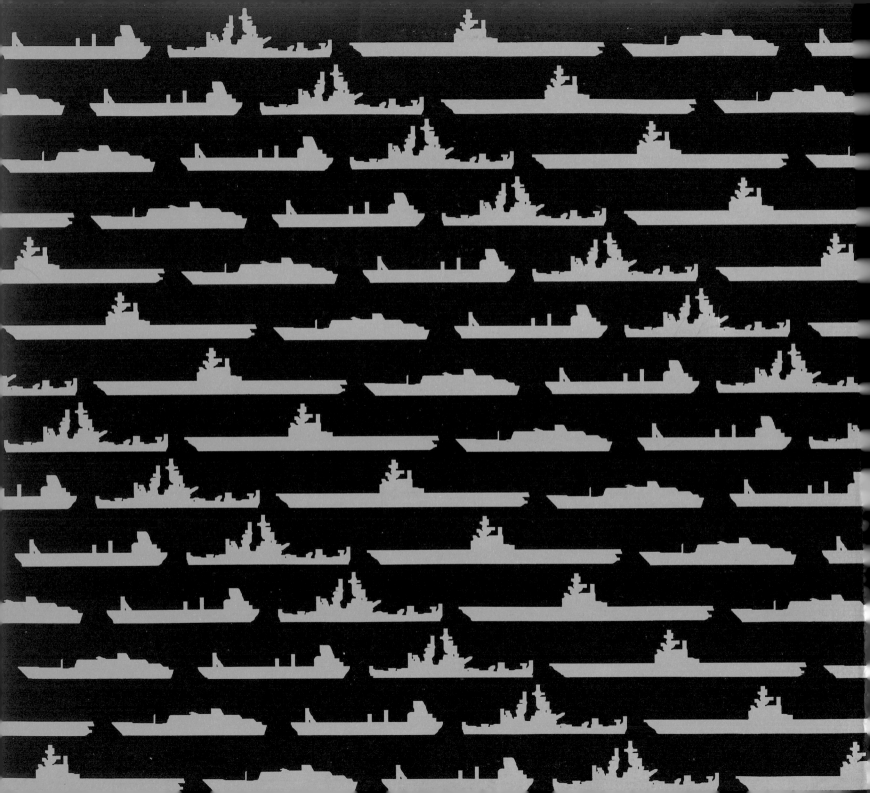